King Arthur Country
In Cornwall

BRENDA DUXBURY
AND
MICHAEL WILLIAMS

The Search for
the Real Arthur

COLIN WILSON

BOSSINEY BOOKS

First published in 1979
by Bossiney Books
St Teath, Bodmin, Cornwall
Typeset and printed in Great Britain by
Penwell Ltd., Parkwood, Callington,
Cornwall

Plate Acknowledgments

Cover by Ray Bishop
Maps by Paul Honeywill
Pages 14, 20, 48 Kerry Mudd
Pages 23-28 Ray Bishop, by courtesy of Hall of Chivalry
Page 84 RNAS Culdrose, Courtesy of Ministry of Defence
Pages 71, 75, 81, 88 John Chard
Pages 73, 82, 83, 85 David Clarke
Pages 76, 78, 79 F.E. Gibson
Pages 29-31 Ronald Youlton
Pages 12, 15 David Cook
All other photographs by Ray Bishop

About Arthur and the Authors

Arthur's fascination is not easily defined. His magnetism down the ages is a curious mixture: fact and fiction, romance and war, chivalry and tragedy are only some of the alluring ingredients. And beyond all these lies the enigma: the impossibility and the probability.

Interestingly, all three authors find themselves close to some of the famous Cornish legends in terms of sheer geography. Brenda Duxbury, who has dug at Castle Killibury, lives high on Bodmin Moor near King Arthur's Hall; Michael Williams who spent ten years at Tintagel, now resides only roughly a couple of miles from Camelford which many people thought to be Arthur's Camelot; while Colin Wilson at Gorran Haven is near the setting of Tristan's legendary leap.

The book is divided into two sections. The first is **King Arthur Country**. This is an exciting exploration of the Arthurian sites in Cornwall and Scilly, including the related legends of King Mark, Tristan and Iseult. Brenda Duxbury and Michael Williams start high on the North Cornish cliffs, amid the castle ruins, and end at Land's End, contemplating the possibility of the lost land of Lyonesse. They explore the sites related to some of the great legends that make Cornwall such a memorable place — not just another English county but a Celtic land apart.

'Ours is not a scholarly excursion,' they admit, 'but we have travelled receptively. We have seen and we have listened . . . and found it a very worthwhile journey.'

Colin Wilson, one of the best-known writers living and working in the Westcountry today, with insight and authority, brings the story to its climax with his **Search for the Real Arthur**. 'Fortunately,' he says, 'Arthur's grave was unmarked; but the tradition of its existence continued to survive in Wales and Cornwall, where the Celts had retreated in the face of the invader. But although the new Angle-land had forgotten Arthur, the Celtic bards remembered him. The legends and the poems proliferated. And Arthur's real conquest — the conquest of the European imagination — began.'

Together with photographs, ancient and modern, drawings and maps, pinpointing the contrasting spots on the Arthurian map of Cornwall, the authors and illustrators have combined to produce this welcome addition for the Arthurian enthusiast — and all lovers of Cornwall.

King Arthur Country
In Cornwall

TINTAGEL CASTLE

The ruins of Tintagel Castle are the heart of the Arthurian romance in Cornwall.

Arthur Mee got it right when he wrote: 'In the evening when the sun is sinking into the Atlantic from something like a flaming battle field we can think it is true about Arthur and his knights. A deep sense of something mysterious comes upon us.'

It's a matter of belief. Cornwall, and the whole world for that matter, have consciously willed the legends to be true. And does it really matter if fact and fiction have become confused? The legends have lived through the hearts and minds of men and women seeking consolation and purpose, for some answer or for some formula in the struggle between good and evil. And the symbolism is as valid today as it has been down the ages.

To many of us it is the ideal that matters, and this great myth — if it be a myth — this great love story, has been a powerful influence, helping to shape literature and music — and sparking ideas and ideals.

We like to think that controversial cleric, Bernard Walke, possibly held the key to it all when he said, 'I do not know what historical evidence there is concerning Tintagel with the Holy Grail legend, but I am convinced that something of spiritual import happened here.'

For those who seek the truth about Arthur, the assumption is that he lived around 500 AD. Unfortunately, Tintagel Castle was not built until the twelfth century.

5

The earliest mention of the Castle in connection with King Arthur appeared about 1145 when Geoffrey of Monmouth published his *History of the Kings of Britain*. This book was an immediate success with Tintagel portrayed as the seat of Gorlois, Duke of Cornwall. It was then Geoffrey of Monmouth who made Tintagel the birthplace of Arthur.

This Welsh Bishop wrote to satisfy the thirst for romance, bravery and chivalry all those years ago, and we wonder if by some magical means he came back today, whether he would be surprised to still find that same thirst and longing. Despite modern education, and our material approach to life, many people today are as super-stitious, or more so, than those Geoffrey of Monmouth was writing for. Julie Welch in a *Sunday Telegraph* feature on superstition reflected, 'Even among some of the well-known people I talked to, there is a feeling that the world is a pretty terrible place at the moment — that superstition is the panacea against its hideousness . . . successful people, whom you would think would be the last to need such reassurance.'

In such a climate, is it surprising that there is still a need for Arthur, for romance, for hero-worship? Superstition might not be mentally respectable today. Arthur, however, has been made respectable by the sheer physical efforts of archaeologists and the enquiring minds of scholars in what has become an international Agatha Christie — a detective operation to identify and place him. Despite it all, he remains a shadowy, elusive personality and is as attractive as ever for these very reasons.

Geoffrey of Monmouth may have updated Arthur by something like six centuries for the benefit of his readers, yet we have kept him in Geoffrey of Monmouth's Medieval setting. Look at the ruins here at Tintagel today, a mere skeleton of the original Norman fortress, but when the Welsh Bishop stood on these cliffs, he was looking at a most up-to-date fortification — a natural setting for an Arthur who had been moved from the sixth to the twelfth century in imagination. An Arthur transformed from a Dark Age chieftain or warrior to a Medieval King with a Medieval castle and all the royal trappings, his loyal warriors changed into chivalrous knights in the brotherhood of the Round Table.

Tintagel Castle ruins▶

A natural setting for King Arthur

This great headland is now almost an island, but in the twelfth century, it was joined to the mainland by a narrow isthmus. When Geoffrey of Monmouth stood here and created the Arthurian geography, he described the access as 'so narrow that three armed knights might hold it against the entire realm of Britain'. For it was on this isthmus that Reginald, Earl of Cornwall, laid the foundations of his Norman castle, with a deep ditch and massive bank topped with a palisade keeping all and sundry at bay. But erosion of centuries of Atlantic onslaught have swept away most of Reginald's work, only the chapel nave and remnants of the Great Hall surviving today.

The Castle's next creator was Richard, Lord of Tintagel, from 1236 to 1272, Earl of Cornwall and King of the Romans, brother of Henry III. If it were not for Arthur, then this Richard would have been the man instinctively linked with Tintagel.

Richard will always be remembered as a great builder. Evidence of his talent is to be found here and at Launceston; while Restormel,

This great headland is almost an island

just outside Lostwithiel, was also Richard's responsibility, but there the building of the stone shell keep was ascribed to his son Edmund.

As far as Tintagel is concerned, it was Richard who built the brace of wards on the mainland and the curtain wall around the courtyard on the headland incorporating the earlier Great Hall. Then a bridge linked the two sections and Richard made further additions, the Iron Gate and the sea wall near the base of the cliffs.

During the 1300s the Castle belonged to the Black Prince. Following his death, decline set in once more through erosion and human neglect. Near the end of the century, however, the Castle was repaired and turned into a prison. But by the 1500s the gap between the headland had widened drastically and the site had become derelict.

Indeed, but for the literary movement of the nineteenth century — with its interest in the Arthurian legends — the Castle would have crumbled into even greater decay. In 1818 Turner, the great English

9

Florence Nightingale Richards

Remains of the Celtic monastery

painter, painted the Castle — a fanciful work perhaps, but powerful and dramatic and full of atmosphere. Other famous characters were fired by the magic of the place: Robert Stephen Hawker, Charles Dickens, Thackeray and Tennyson, were all touched by Tintagel.

A big factor in the Castle's preservation was the arrival of the new vicar in 1851, the Reverend R.B. Kinsman, who was to hold the living for more than forty years. He set about shaping a new path to the headland. In 1820 there had been a huge landslide — debris cluttering the landscape and access being extremely difficult. Kinsman resurrected the ancient office of Constable of the Castle and delighted in wearing an imposing scarlet and gold attire 'when conducting visitors thither'.

For many years the keys of Tintagel Castle were entrusted to one Florence Nightingale Richards. 'A short dark woman, a throwback to the ancient British type,' is how one contemporary remembered her. A personality, who might have stepped out of the Arthurian pages, Florence lived with her mother in a cottage, known as Castle

13

A reconstruction of Tintagel Castle by Kerry Mudd

Cottage, which today is the bookshop and ticket office for the Castle at the bottom of the Vale of Avalon, the name given to the valley leading to the cove. She had several keys and would only part with any of them with the strict instruction to lock the Castle door 'on entering and departing'. Often though, she braved the worst storms to show visitors the ruins and she was especially fond of pointing out a cavity in the rock in sight of the church where, she claimed, Arthur planted one foot, the other being poised on the distant church tower!

One of the most dramatic methods of approaching Tintagel Castle is by walking the cliff path to the Castle Keep. So if you're on wheels, park your car on the cliffs by the church, dedicated to St Materiana who, according to tradition, evangelised parts of Cornwall around 500 AD. The present Norman church is thought to stand on the site of a small Celtic Oratory which — if true — means that Christian

Mining for silver at Tintagel

worship has been practised on this spot for over 1400 years.

At Rogationtide services have been held at the Chapel of St Jullia, the Norman Chapel on the Castle, probably built on the site of a much earlier church belonging to a Celtic monastic settlement. This settlement was almost certainly founded by St Julian or St Juliot. Maybe starting with a simple oratory, it soon became a flourishing community of monks who lived in groups of small cells, and it was these monks who built the first bank and ditch to defend the island. This evidence that the island had been fortified long before Reginald started work, must have encouraged Geoffrey of Monmouth to name Tintagel as Arthur's castle. The monastic settlement may have been the 'Rosnant' mentioned in several early Irish sources, for the name means 'headland by the valley' — a fitting description of Tintagel. Interestingly it has been dated directly to Arthur's time in the later fifth century AD by fragments of imported Mediterranean pottery

found in the ruins.

Although the Norman Castle may not have belonged to Arthur in time, these Celtic monks worked and worshipped here in the same fifth century.

If you have a head for heights, our advice is climb those many hundred steps yourself. Out there on that mighty headland, you not only come to the heart of the Arthurian romance, but you also feel the heart beats of Cornwall herself. To call any part of Cornwall the best is sheer presumption, for Cornwall has many moods and meanings. She is different things to different people. Only a painter's eye or a poet's words can truly describe this chunk of Cornwall, and who better to do that than the Poet Laureate, Sir John Betjeman, who lives not many miles down the coast? 'The black jagged slate,' he has written, 'of which the Norman Castle is built, the loop holes for arrows, the mighty inaccessible cliffs of black slate, the way above the tide line, the slate has been scooped by wind and rain into ridges

16

and basins, the short wind-shorn turf, the touching remains of early Christian cells and the ever present merciless roll of the heaving Atlantic . . . all lend strength to the legend . . .'

A dramatic fortress then on a magical piece of Cornish coastline seemed to Geoffrey of Monmouth a fitting birthplace for King Arthur. The story is that Uther Pendragon, King of Britain, became infatuated with Ygraine, wife of Gorlois, Duke of Cornwall, and rated the most beautiful woman in the kingdom. The King's interest in her was such that her husband kept her virtually a prisoner at Tintagel and refused to return to Court. An infuriated Uther descended on Cornwall. Such was his longing for the woman that Merlin, the Wizard, prescribed a magic brew enabling him to look the twin brother of Gorlois. Thus disguised, he had no difficulty in entering the Castle and that night he slept with Ygraine. As a result Arthur was conceived. Gorlois was defeated and killed in battle with Uther's army, and his wife, now liberated, became Queen of Britain.

Arthur — or his myth — clings tenaciously to Tintagel. Though scholars clash on Arthur and his authenticity, local tradesmen have had no inhibition or hesitation: Arthurian names have been given to all kinds of commercial enterprises. Understandably not everybody approves. 'At Tintagel,' reflected Ronald Duncan, 'we see nothing now but the commercial exploitation of these myths. It is the achievement of the twentieth century to turn a poem into a bazaar; Isolde into an ashtray.'

Luckily, though, Ronald Duncan isn't strictly accurate, for commercialization has not yet scarred much of this Tintagel coastline.

MERLIN'S CAVE

Many heroes have a Supernatural quality. Often their birth is surrounded with a mysterious and magical aura. Arthur has a larger than Life personality and some writers have even suggested that he was conceived of the Gods.

So it is only natural that there should be a second version of his birth, one charged with magic and supernatural powers, and if you stand on the cliffs at Tintagel on a storm-scarred day, with an angry Atlantic climbing the walls of the cliffs, you can easily picture Merlin's acceptance of the babe from the ocean.

Whichever version you accept, Merlin will always be alive at Tintagel. Lying directly below the ruins is Merlin's Cave. Full of atmosphere and drama, and in certain lights possessing an almost theatrical quality, this, the most famous cave in Cornwall, pierces the great cliff, cutting right through to a small rocky beach on the other side of the headland. Clamber through, over the rocks, at low water, but watch out for the rising tide.

It is no coincidence that Cornwall is sometimes known as the land of Merlin, for apart from its Supernatural quality in places, we cannot begin to understand King Arthur until we know Merlin and know of his influence on Arthur, the boy and King.

Assuming we accept the human conception of Arthur, one legend tells us that Merlin claimed the child and chose the name Arthur. He then dispatched him to be brought up secretly by Ector and his wife with their young son Kay. Moreover it was a secret well kept by Merlin and Ector, for not even Arthur knew the truth about his

Looking out from Merlin's Cave

The Sword in the Stone by Kerry Mudd

parentage. He was only two when his true father, Uther Pendragon, died and there followed nearly thirteen years of interregnum. Then, when Arthur was approaching fifteen years of age, Merlin called the nobility of the land to London around Christmas, assuring them that the identity of the rightful King would be revealed. Malory, whose *Morte d' Arthur,* written in the fifteenth century, was printed on Caxton's press, sets the scene in a London churchyard: 'a great stone foursquare, like unto a marble stone; and in midst thereof was like an anvil of steel a foot on high, and therein stuck a fair sword naked by the point, and letters there were written in gold about the sword that said thus: — Whoso pulleth out this sword of this stone and anvil is rightwise King born of all England.'

Many attempted to draw the sword. None succeeded. However when the young Arthur came he drew it easily, whereupon Ector told Arthur that he had proved himself to be the rightful King. Furthermore Ector revealed that he was not Arthur's true father.

An astonished Arthur was made King, much to the chagrin of many powerful lords who disliked the idea of being ruled by a mere boy. Merlin, for his part, told them the truth, but many refused to believe him and it took Arthur several years to prove himself and be accepted as the natural King.

In time Arthur's barons urged him to marry. The King was entranced by Guinevere whom he regarded as the bravest and fairest woman in the whole nation. Merlin, with his gift of second sight, endeavoured to warn the King, but Arthur failed to understand or respond. So Arthur and Guinevere were married at a magnificent wedding ceremony and feast at the Court of Camelot.

But a shadow was to fall over this event with the unexpected appearance of the Lady of the Lake. Merlin, incredibly, fell in love with her on sight; unfortunately she disliked Merlin intensely, yet somehow concealed her true feelings. So when she left Camelot, Merlin went with her. Turning his own magical powers against him, she sealed him in a tomb in the perilous forest. Merlin vanished from the scene. Arthur had gained a wife, albeit the wrong one, and worse still had lost his Supernatural adviser.

This, though, is only one version of the story. Therefore you will meet Merlin again in our journey — our search for Arthur.

There was almost certainly never an historical Merlin. But he gives the whole story a Supernatural quality. Writers have often reinforced their heroes with an Occult aide, and Merlin uses his magical powers at the very outset by arranging Arthur's birth at Tintagel. Yet curiously, as many modern clairvoyants claim, he could not see for himself.

THE HALL OF CHIVALRY

Cornwall has the ability to surprise, and even astonish, and at Tintagel there is an Arthurian surprise for many people hiding behind a shop front. For beyond it are two halls, conceived by Frederick Thomas Glasscock. They may be manmade, but in spirit and substance they are as Cornish as Rough Tor or Barras Nose.

More than fifty different types of stone were used to construct the Hall of Chivalry and every one a Cornish stone, ranging from slate and granite to serpentine and porphyry, tourmaline and greenstone. Granite came in from the widely scattered regions of the county: from St Breward and Redruth, from Sheffield and Carn Brea, from Withiel and Castle-an-Dinas, from Luxulyan and the Lizard, from Gunnislake and Rough Tor. There are seventy-three stained glass windows — fit for a cathedral — showing the heraldry of the Arthurian knights with their symbolic interpretations. The virtue of humility, for example, is represented by the handle and the pommel of a sword; the crown of humility is said to be pure gold with a black background implying self-obliteration; the precept in Spurgeon's words being — 'the higher a man is in the grace the lower will he be in his own esteem.'

Everything here is based on the Arthurian romances. This was, at one time, the headquarters of the Fellowship of the Order of the Round Table, an organization conceived by Frederick Thomas Glasscock. A millionaire — partner in the famous custard firm of Monkhouse and Glasscock — he came to Cornwall to retire, but instead, falling in love with the romances and seeing their commercial possibilities, he founded the order and started reaping a second fortune. He died in 1934, aboard the *Queen Mary*, on his way to the United States.

Some people may say the Hall of Chivalry is overdone and is not

Stained glass window in Hall of Chivalry▶

▲Reproduction of Round Table . . .

. . . King Arthur's throne▶

their cup of tea, but it is for many a door opening to the whole Arthurian theme. And if the ghost of Frederick Thomas Glasscock lurks in the village today, we suspect he is well pleased that so many young visitors are introduced to King Arthur and the Knights of the Round Table through this building, his brain child all those years ago.

The Round Table was an inspired idea for it demolished any disputes as to which knight sat above another. A Cornish carpenter apparently suggested the idea of a Round Table, and then made it for Arthur. As the King enlisted so many knights, the Table was divided into sections so that it could be taken to pieces and reassembled wherever the King went.

Standing amid all the beautiful Cornish craftsmanship in the Hall of Chivalry at Tintagel, you realize the story of the Cornish carpenter creating the Round Table could have been very plausible.

Another theory links the Round Table to the Holy Grail. Joseph of Arimathea, fired by the Holy Spirit, set up a Grail Table in com-

memoration of the historic Last Supper, when Judas Iscariot disappeared into the night to betray Jesus. This treachery was the reason why one place was always left vacant at the Grail Table.

In time, the Grail Table became the model for the Round Table, and though it seated as many as 150 knights, one place always remained vacant — but for a different, higher reason — this was the Siege Perilous, otherwise known as the Dangerous Seat. Only the ultimate hero could dine here — the knight who was to win the Holy Grail.

So the Round Table, symbolising the brotherhood of Christ's disciples, became the focus for King Arthur's fellowship of knights who wandered the countryside in search of adventure, to vie with each other and to test themselves to the limit in courage, strength and virtue righting the wrongs of the world.

Camelot, the Court of Arthur, is about many things, but it is certainly about Romance, and a good deal of the fighting of the knights is for the sake of a lady. Often she inspires the knight to these feats of heroism — and through them he reaches the fulfilment of integrity.

A female theme, in fact, runs through the legends. Yet another theory is that Arthur acquired the Round Table through marrying Guinevere, the Queen bringing it to Camelot as her dowry.

Whichever version is right, the Round Table remains at the heart of the Arthur story and a splendid example of democratic dining, and, of course, deeper than any democracy, it stands for wholeness and perfection.

There is a fine collection of Arthurian literature in the Hall — sadly, though, some of the best volumes were auctioned in London — and several paintings by William Hatherell R.I. Using Malory's *Morte d'Arthur* as the basis of his work, Hatherell takes us through King Arthur's life. You see him as a babe being handed to Merlin at the Postern Gate at Tintagel Castle; you see him being offered the magical sword Excalibur; the knighting of Sir Galahad; Lancelot being refused the sight of the Holy Grail but Sir Galahad beholding the vision. You see also the rescue of Guinevere from the flames and the battle between Arthur and Sir Mordred before the King passes to the Vale of Avalon.

Arthur being offered 'Excalibur' by the Lady of the Lake — painting by Hatherell▶

The entrance of Sir Galahad to court — Hatherell

Today this building is used for Masonic Lodge meetings. Colour and light make great impact. The stones are astonishing in their variety, subtle shades, contrasting differences. Green, blue, grey, brown, buff, cream, golden, pink, silver-grey, white, red, black and yellow — you begin to comprehend Cornwall's mineral wealth — and the windows are coloured in such a way as to reflect their virtues. Those portraying the highest spiritual qualities are brightest. The colours also correspond with the rainbow: purple at one end, golden red at the other. Shading and lighting, allied to curtains stretching from the ceiling to the floor, give the impression that you are moving from comparative darkness into a beautiful and brilliant glow.

Ronald Youlton who still lives in Tintagel remembers when Frederick Glasscock first came to the village. He was a teenager when the retired millionaire saw a display of Monkhouse and Glasscock's jellies and custard powders in the window of his father's

Frederick Glasscock knighting a pilgrim

Ready for opening ceremony 1933

grocer's shop — a display that also included the sword Excalibur and the Round Table, which first caught the imagination of Frederick Glasscock.

Ronald Youlton recalled: 'He built a small hall at first, about 1930, but when his Fellowship of the Order of the Knights of the Round Table flourished, a larger hall was needed.

'You could join the Order as a Searcher if you were a child. A teenager could be a pilgrim for a small fee. You could then progress through twelve months probation to qualify as a knight, as long as you were proposed and seconded.' You were then presented with a book on the Fellowship and other literature for a small cost.

'The King Arthur business snowballed and on 5 June 1933 over five hundred people came from all parts for the opening of the new grand Hall of Chivalry, built behind the earlier King Arthur's Hall. This was consecrated by the Bishop of Truro and Frederick Glasscock was well on the way to making his second million. He went to

Searchers, Pilgrims and knights at the Round Table

America and launched the idea successfully over there and on his return had to employ secretaries to deal with the growing correspondence.'

'What sort of person was Frederick Glasscock?' we asked.

'He was short, very precise and domineering — a self made man who behaved rather like a little god. But he was a great benefactor to Tintagel providing the men's club, tennis courts, roller skating, starting scout and guide troops. So most people in the village were prepared to go along with him.'

Ronald Youlton, who himself started as a Pilgrim in the Order, went on to describe the knighting ceremony: 'The new knight would be suitably attired for the ceremony while those already knighted wore robes of blue or red according to their rank, whether knights of the sword or sceptre. The principles of the Order were read from a scroll, prayers were said, oaths made. The ceremony started in semi-darkness until the sword Excalibur was drawn from the scabbard with great flourish and Glasscock (in the role of King Arthur) struck the new knight on the shoulder, giving him his name: Sir Galahad, perhaps, Sir Lancelot or Sir Bedivere.

BOSSINEY MOUND

Bossiney is not Tintagel. Though one ends and the other begins without obvious gap on the corkscrewing coastal road to Boscastle, Bossiney has an identity of its own. It may have neither church nor monument, but times were when it was greater in importance, days when Bossiney and Trevena — the old name for Tintagel — were a united Borough, boasting a Mayor and Corporation, a seal and mace, sending not one but two Members of Parliament to London.

There is one lovely story about a certain Mayor of Bossiney. He was a farmer and no scholar. When the Sheriff arrived one day with a writ, Mr Mayor was busy thatching a rick. Determined not to lose time, he proceeded to read the document upside down. The Sheriff, attempting to be helpful, pointed out this fact, only to be promptly told: 'Sir, the Mayor of Bossiney can read upside down if he wants!'

The village of Bossiney grew around what is today a hump on the landscape. Cloaked in gorse and hemlock, cocksfoot and bracken, Bossiney Mound stands alongside the squat Methodist Chapel on the eastern side of the road. Moreover, history and legend combine to give it a special significance in the story of North Cornwall. It was a castle, used for defensive purposes until the building of Tintagel Castle, and its architect was Robert, Earl of Mortain, a half-brother of William the Conqueror. To this Mound traders brought their slaves for auction. Here, too, Cornishmen raised their right hand to send Sir Francis Drake to Parliament.

It was Sabine Baring-Gould, that many sided squire and parson from Lewtrenchard, just over the Cornwall-England border, who wove Bossiney Mound into the Arthurian tapestry. 'According to Cornish tradition,' he said, 'King Arthur's golden Round Table lies deep in the earth buried under this earthen circular mound; only on Midsummer night does it rise, and then the flash of light from it for the moment illumines the sky, after which the golden table sinks again. At the end of the world it will come to the surface again and be carried to Heaven, and the Saints will sit and eat at it, and Christ

Bossiney Mound

will serve them.'

The curious thing is that people, including one of us, have seen a strange inexplicable light here on Midsummer Eve: a light suddenly appearing inside one of the Chapel windows only a few yards away — a glow rather than a single shaft of electricity — like a patch of moorland mist. It vanished as dramatically and inexplicably as it had appeared. In the words of one witness: 'We *know* we saw something. I'll always believe it was something to do with the legend. Why tonight? And why so near the Mound?'

ROCKY VALLEY

Down the hill beyond Bossiney lies Rocky Valley which was said to be the haunt of one of the last pairs of Cornish Choughs. With his glossy black plumage, scarlet legs and long, curved scarlet beak, the Chough is bigger than the Jackdaw. He is, of course, more than a mere bird to the patriotic Cornishman. He is the symbol of the County. Sad to say, the Chough is now doomed to extinction: the

Cornish Chough at least. And even he is linked to legend in that when the Cornish Chough goes, Cornwall's prosperity will go with him. Superstition however gives us a glimmer of hope. Deep back in our folklore there is a notion Arthur did not die that day in the battle at Slaughter Bridge. Instead the Chough incarnated the King's soul — and Arthur will come again.

SLAUGHTER BRIDGE

Near the old Camelford station, a curving road crosses Slaughter Bridge.

You can rarely see the beauty of a bridge by simply standing on it, and Slaughter Bridge is no exception. Look at it from the nearby field and you'll realize it's very old: not arched but constructed over flat stones on piers, very much like that famous clapper Postbridge on Dartmoor. There may be bigger and more beautiful Cornish bridges, but Slaughter Bridge is a gem with a character of its own.

This is an essential part of any Arthurian tour of Cornwall, for it strides the River Camel in its infancy, and the Camel hereabouts is often said to have been the site of the Battle of Camlann.

Malory tells the dramatic story of Arthur's last battle when he was forced to fight his bastard son Mordred who had betrayed him. It was so furious a conflict that in the end only two of the knights of the Round Table were left alive. Arthur knew his time had come. 'I am come to mine end,' he said and he slew Mordred with his own spear, but the dying traitor raised his sword and struck his father on the head piercing through the helmet to the brain. So Arthur had killed Mordred with his own hands as he had sworn to do.

Up stream in a sequestered nook lies the stone, embroidered in moss and strange lettering. It is called Arthur's grave but it is almost certainly that of another Celtic chieftain.

And if the stone slab here does commemorate some historic battle, it is more likely to have been one fought in 825 during the Saxon Conquest of Cornwall.

Rocky Valley ▶

34

Ambition, rivalry and a question of succession are the classic ingredients for trouble, and as Arthur advanced into old age, this proved to be so. Mordred — in some versions he is Arthur's nephew — was highly ambitious, and he was building up support among the younger brigade; jealousy and a desire to achieve independence motivated them. It was the age-old conflict between the 'young bloods' and the 'old guard' who backed Arthur. Mordred, in a sentence, succeeded in dividing the Round Table — it was no longer a full circle, rather a semi-circle and therefore that much weaker through dissention. There was a further complication in that Lancelot, deeply in love with the Queen, sided with Mordred.

CAMELFORD — CAMELOT?

Camelford, by virtue of its name, must come into any Arthurian reckoning in Cornwall, yet, on the surface, there is no Camelot quality. Until the introduction of some industry in recent years, it was basically a quiet country town. Today the growth of tourism has made it a difficult traffic spot at weekends at the height of the holiday season. Its sheer geography, however, puts it firmly on the

◄Slaughter Bridge . . .   . . . called Arthur's Grave▼

Arthurian map: only six miles from Tintagel, and very near Slaughter Bridge. On the northern fringe of Bodmin Moor, Camelford is set on a steep hill, falling to a small river — this is the Camel in its infancy, another fact which makes Arthur and his Court hang in the air and in our imagination.

It would need a whole library of books to tell of Arthur's adventures, how he brought peace to Britain. But as each calendar followed another, his fame spread across land and sea to the extent that the bravest and noblest knights came to his Court in the hope that by their deeds of courage and gentleness they might win a place at his Round Table.

In our imagination we can picture the Court in its Medieval setting: celebrations in the Great Hall, ladies in shining silks, immaculate knights, minstrels playing, dining and wining, the crackle of log fires, great doors opening and closing.

Yet for all the elegance, all the idealism and heroism, Arthur's story is a tragedy. Despite his brilliant career, his beautiful wife Guinevere and all the trappings of Camelot, he is doomed. The passionate love between Guinevere and ironically his champion and friend, Lancelot, destroys his happiness, plunges his kingdom into war and shatters the Round Table. There is the ultimate betrayal by Mordred. Whatever one may have thought of the film technically, *Camelot*, on the big screen, was a very sad story.

It was the Medieval French writers , like Chrétien de Troyes, who first attributed the name Camelot to Arthur's Court. But they were vague about its location. Before them, Geoffrey of Monmouth had Arthur's principal seat in Wales at Caerleon and the Welsh Triads at Kelli Wic in Cornwall. Malory took it further east to Winchester, and Leland in the sixteenth century favoured Cadbury Castle in Somerset.

But lying as it does near to Slaughter Bridge, Tintagel only five miles as the Cornish Chough flew, Camelford on the River Camel has always been a favourite in the search for Camelot.

KILLIBURY CASTLE

In our Cornish search for Arthur's Court, we followed the River Camel down to Wadebridge where the moorland waters taste the salt of the sea at the head of the estuary. It is the Welsh Triads, the earliest source for the location of Arthur's legendary Courts, that bring us here to Killibury Castle. They mention 'Kelli Wic in Cornwall' as one of three sites attributed to the Courts of Arthur, the other two being in Wales and the north.

Did these writers have an actual place in mind or was it just an imaginary court for the hero of their story?

It seems likely from the evidence that Kelli Wic existed but whether Arthur actually lived there, or whether Kelli Wic was Killibury, we may never know. Most nineteenth century historians favoured Callington, whereas from 1900 onwards the die seems to have been cast in favour of Killibury, but the evidence is very tenuous.

However, Killibury Castle is real enough. But ask a local the way and he will say, 'Where? Oh, Kelly Rounds, you mean!'

The Rounds lie above Wadebridge off the Camelford Road on a lane leading from Three Holes Cross towards Dinham's Bridge. Today, you would be forgiven for not recognising it as an Iron Age hillfort for only half of it remains and this half is covered with undergrowth and bushes. Nor is its setting so dramatic as many a Cornish Cliff Castle or prominent hillfort built during what must have been unsettled and aggressive times.

However, from its siting on a flat-topped hill, the view is impressive. In one direction, you can look right down on the upper reaches of the Camel estuary as it flows out to join the Atlantic. This was one of Cornwall's main routeways in time past, for travellers crossing by boat from Wales or Ireland would avoid the perilous rounding of Land's End by sea and navigate as far as possible up the Camel before taking the land route across the peninsula to join the Fowey River near Lostwithiel where they could re-embark for the south coast of England or the Continent.

Turn completely around and you can see southwards towards Bodmin and the Moor. Were it not for the trees, you would see the neighbouring hillfort in Pencarrow Woods. In fact several other hillforts were probably visible to the Iron Age inhabitants of Killibury.

Originally a circular earthwork consisting of two concentric banks and ditches, today only one side of Kelly Rounds remains. The other side has been ploughed out and a pig farm now flourishes where the prehistoric fortifications once stood. In fact the road cuts the fort in half.

In the drought of 1976, the two rings stood out clearly from the air, even the ploughed-out southern ditches showing up as crop marks from above. I was lucky enough to be part of the team from the County Archaeological Society that excavated a small section of the fort near the south east inner rampart. We found the post holes of Iron Age timber buildings and the base of a clay oven, but at the back of everyone's mind lurked a thought. Would we find any evidence that Killibury was inhabited during the time of Arthur?

Since the dramatic discoveries at Cadbury in Somerset where Leslie Alcock uncovered a gate tower and timber hall built during the Arthurian period, whenever an Iron Age hillfort is excavated, archaeologists are keen to see whether the ramparts were rebuilt and the fort inhabited during this Dark Age period. Where legend or earlier texts have linked the site with Arthur, then such archaeological evidence can add a little more fact to the confused realms of myth and folklore that surround the whole story of Arthur.

At Killibury no hall was unearthed nor gate tower, but two pieces of pottery, orange-red in colour, were found in the ploughsoil. These are known to be part of an amphora or amphorae which came all the way from the eastern Mediterranean some time between the late fifth and early seventh century AD.

Slight evidence to be sure for the occupation of Killibury during the Arthurian period, but an important chunk of Cornish history all the same.

And on the subject of genuine history, was there a real Arthur? The odds are that there is *some* basis of truth in the legends. At the time he was thought to have lived, the Roman Empire had collapsed, the Roman army had withdrawn and the Roman province was left to fend for itself against the Saxon incursions.

Although Gildas, writing a hundred years later about the defeat of the Saxons at Badon Hill in 500 AD, tells of the great peace that followed, he doesn't mention Arthur as the leader, but then he doesn't mention any leader. However, Nennius, two hundred years later, has Arthur as *dux bellorum*, warleader rather than king, firmly established as the victor of twelve battles culminating in the triumph of Badon Hill, where he himself slew one thousand of the enemy. Arthur had already acquired the prowess of a legendary hero.

Medieval man was certain Arthur ruled but scholars in the Age of Reason were sceptical. Gibbon, though, had faith in an historical Arthur. One fact is as plain as the often-quoted pikestaff: the Saxon

Castle-an-Dinas

infiltration of the Westcountry was halted and almost certainly that opposition stemmed from inspiring leadership — maybe someone far removed from our legendary concept of Arthur in shimmering armour — but, at least, a leader with spirit and a sound sense of strategy, a guerrilla-warfare fighter perhaps like Tito in Yugoslavia in the 1939-45 war.

CASTLE-AN-DINAS

Another hillfort with Arthurian connections is Castle-an-Dinas, which has been suggested as the King's Hunting Lodge. This is a most impressive Cornish Iron Age hillfort, situated on a prominent hilltop near St Columb with extensive views of the landscape. And the silhouette of these defences against the skyline can be seen from miles around. Banks and ditches were constructed to circle the hilltop probably with a wooden palisade topping the innermost, and from here the defenders of the fort could bombard their invaders with sling stones.

It had the facilities to house an army of soldiers and by virtue of its geography, seven hundred feet high, it must have been rated one of the strongest fortifications in the Westcountry.

JESUS WELL

Though Arthur has grown into a big bone of contention, most writers and scholars *are* agreed on one point. Arthur's quest for the Holy Grail is central to the whole Arthurian platform. Legend has it that the Chalice, used by Christ at the Last Supper, was brought to this country by Joseph of Arimathea, who as a merchant traded with Cornwall for tin. But did Christ himself — as a young lad — come to Cornwall? We like to think so, for there is a tradition that the young Jesus came with Joseph on one tin collecting expedition. Place, Fowey, St Just in Roseland, Looe Island, all lay claim to being the site of Christ's landing in Cornwall. But only one place bears his name on the map. The Camel Estuary version is that the boy came ashore at St Minver to get fresh water supplies for the ship. Anyway the Jesus Well, by St Minver, is marked by that name on the appropriate Ordnance Survey Map and interestingly it provides a water supply to this day. Indeed some believed its water had magical qualities. The Quiller-Couches on a visit in the 1890s discovered that children suffering from whooping cough were still taken to drink the waters . . . 'pins were dropped in for the telling of fortunes and money was cast into its depths for the same reason . . .'

Malory gave a vivid description of the Holy Grail coming to the Court of Camelot when Arthur and the Knights were seated at the Round Table, dining on Whit Sunday: 'Then anon they heard the cracking and crying of thunder, that the palace should all to-drive (burst to pieces). So in the midst of the blast entered a sunbeam, more clearer by seven times than ever they saw day, and all they were alighted of (illumined by) the grace of the Holy Ghost. Then every knight began to behold other, and every saw other, by their seeming, fairer than they ever were before. Not for then there was no knight that might speak one word a great while, and so they looked every man on other as they had been dumb.

'Then entered into the hall the Holy Grail covered with white samite, but there was none that might see it nor whom that bare it. And there was all the hall fulfilled with good odours and every knight had such meats and drinks as he best loved in this world.

'And when the Holy Grail had been borne through the Hall, then the Holy vessel departed suddenly, that they wist not where it became. Then had they all breath to speak, and then the king yielded thankings to God of His good grace that He had sent them.'

The legends of the Holy Grail resemble the Cornish landscape on a misty day — wrapped in an atmosphere of mystery. They somehow hold a secret that remains seemingly for ever beyond our mental, physical and spiritual grasp. Generations of writers have endeavoured to pin that special something to paper. It has been called 'the perfection of Paradise', and 'an abundance of the sweetness of the world'. It has been referred to as 'the source of valour undismayed', and 'the spring-head of endeavour'. But perhaps Richard Cavendish came closest to the secret when he wrote: 'The inner mystery of the Grail cannot be explained because it is "that which the heart of man cannot conceive nor tongue relate".'

As we have researched and written and travelled both physically across Cornwall and in our imagination, we have perhaps learnt two things. Arthur is all about a search, and, at the heart of it all, is an attempt by the individual to find his or her best self.

The tragedy underlying this great legend is Lancelot's passion for the King's wife. Lancelot, who had come to Arthur's rescue again and again, is, of course, a key figure in the Arthurian cast. For all his skills and accomplishment, Lancelot, the undisputed best of the knights, falls short. For his obsession with Guinevere deprives him of a coveted honour of winning the Grail and, even worse, ultimately reduces the whole Arthurian kingdom to ruins.

ST ENDELLION

You cannot easily escape Arthur in Cornwall. Like John Wesley you are constantly reminded of him, and he often has the ability to surprise. We, for instance, learnt something, that surprised us, on this Arthurian journey across Cornwall. We have both known St Endellion for a good many years, yet only recently did we discover an Arthurian connection. St Endellion, perched high between Delabole and Polzeath, we rate one of the loveliest, uncluttered churches in all Cornwall. She almost seems to have grown out of this windswept North Cornish landscape, an impression that may be due to the fact that she was built with Cornish granite and local stone; while the tower was shaped from Lundy Island granite.

What has Arthur to do with this church, you may wonder. Admittedly the view across the beautiful but menacing coastline leads naturally to Tintagel Head. Well, St Endelienta, to whom this church was dedicated, was the goddaughter of Arthur himself.

St Endelienta was the daughter of a Welsh King, living in the sixth century. It is said all his twenty-four children were canonized. She was a sister to St Minefreda, St Udy, St Teath and others including St Julian of Tintagel to whom churches in the district were dedicated. St Endelienta lived as a hermit in the valley approximately half a mile from where the church stands today. Tradition has it that she lived solely on milk from a cow. One day the cow strayed onto some neighbouring land and the unfriendly neighbour, Lord of Tretinney, killed the animal. In angry revenge her godfather — King Arthur — slew him. Yet St Endelienta miraculously brought him back to life.

The precise geography too has an interesting genesis. Shortly before the end of her earthly life St Endelienta requested that her body be placed on a cart drawn by bullocks or heifers — and that they should be allowed to go free — and that she should be buried where they stopped. They drew the cart and corpse to the top of the hill where today the church stands.

DOZMARY POOL

Now our journey takes us inland to Bodmin Moor. Mary Yelland, peering out of the coach window in the opening chapter of Daphne du Maurier's novel *Jamaica Inn*, set a century and a half ago, saw '. . . mile upon mile of bleak moorland, dark and untraversed, rolling like a desert land to some unseen horizon!' The Moor, in fact, stretches twelve miles north to south and eleven miles east to west.

Just over a mile from the four walls of Jamaica Inn lies Dozmary Pool, a saucer-like depression to the south west of the Fowey valley,

St Endellion ▶

Dozmary Pool . . .

a mile in circumference and 500 yards across.

There was an old tradition that Dozmary Pool was bottomless
— a theory too that sticks had been carried subterraneously to
Falmouth Harbour. In reality, it's surprisingly shallow. Yet its
strange beauty makes it a natural setting for the ghostly and the
magical; almost inevitably the legends of Tregeagle and the sword
Excalibur have grown out of this silent sheet of water. C.E.
Vulliamy, touring Cornwall, in the 1920s, perceptively wrote, 'It
could not be otherwise. The very passage of cloud and shadow,
of mist and darkness over its face, the luminous forms that move
phantasmally over its waters, would suggest miracles and marvels
to the least imaginative mind.'

Of this Moorland scene Vulliamy said: 'Nowhere else on earth are
there landscapes more austerely beautiful, more wonderful in their
changes of mood and colour, or more splendid in outline. The Pool

46

. . . a natural setting for the ghostly

in its placid moods, when it becomes a mirror reflecting the forms
of moor and cloud, has a charm so powerful, yet so elusive, that it
can only be conveyed to you in pictures: the limits of descriptive
writing are soon exhausted.'

John Tregeagle, an unjust steward, was charged — by the spirits
— for his misdeeds, and was sentenced to bail out Dozmary with a
leaky limpet-shell. Tregeagle was so tortured by the impossibility
of his task that he fled to Roche Rock, where, hammering and howling on the door of the chapel, he begged the Saints to grant him
forgiveness and admission. Children of past generations were told
that storm noises were really Tregeagle and his hell hounds out
hunting. Hence the old Cornish expression: 'Howling like a
Tregeagle'.

Dozmary is reputed to be the place where Sir Bedivere grudgingly
threw away the magical sword Excalibur — though some scholars

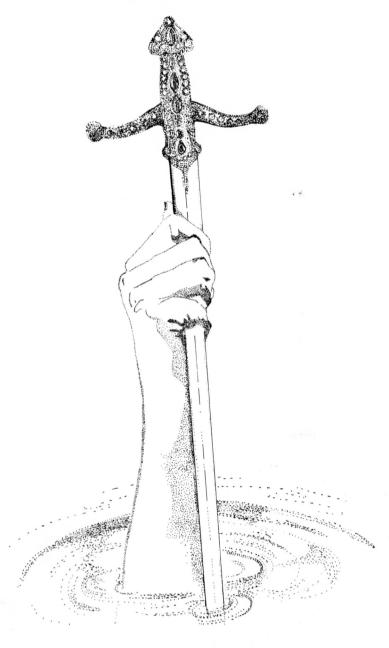

regard Loe Pool near Helston as the more likely setting.

After the battle of Camlann, Sir Bedivere carried the dying Arthur away and Arthur ordered Bedivere to throw the sword Excalibur into a lake close by. Bedivere hesitated, reluctant to throw away such a sword, and hid it instead. When he returned to the King, Arthur asked him what he had seen. 'Nothing', answered Bedivere. Arthur knowing that his instructions had not been carried out, ordered him once again to do his bidding. Once again, Bedivere tried to fool the King. But the third time he did as he was asked. As the sword arced over the lake, 'there came an arm and a hand, and took it and cleight (seized) it, and shook it thrice and brandished, and then vanished with the sword into the water.'

And so Excalibur, which had originally been the gift of the Lady of the Lake, vanished in the same way as it had come.

The Arthurian romances are laced with symbolism and among the most symbolic is the cross-shaped hilt of the swords of the Christian knights. This stood for religious belief and was often used as a sacred emblem upon which oaths were taken and which sometimes reminded the knights of their vows.

And Excalibur with its symbolism lives on today in Cornwall. The most moving part of the Cornish Gorsedd — the annual gathering of the Bards — is when the assembled re-affirm their loyalty on the replica of the great sword. The bards move forward and those in front touch the sword; while those unable to reach it lay their hands on the shoulders of those in front, thus creating a human chain from every Bard to Excalibur.

KING ARTHUR'S HALL

As the number of Arthurian legends increased, so too did his alleged superhuman powers and gradually strange features in the Cornish landscape were attributed to him. Some have been shaped by nature, like Arthur's Bed, his Cup and Saucer, his Chair and Oven. But among the manmade sites King Arthur's Hall, on Downs that also bear his name high on Bodmin Moor, must rank among the most mysterious.

Nobody, for certain, knows its origin — when or why these banks were built. They stand alone, rectangular on the skyline, roughly

CORNWALL

N

Land's
End

St. Michael's Mount   Malpas

Merlyn Rock

Mounts Bay   Loe Pool

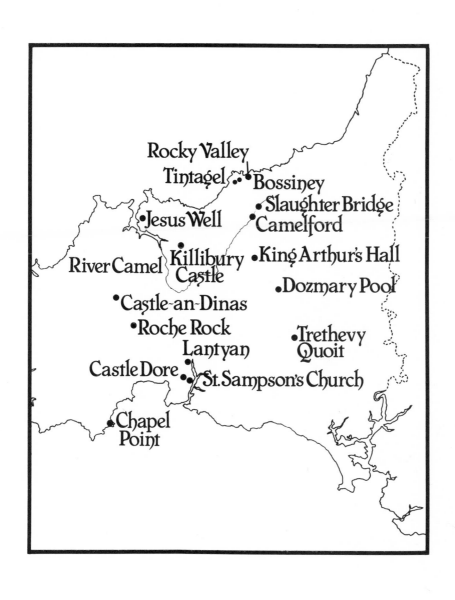

fifty yards long and twenty yards wide, now weathered down to about five feet in height. Today the interior is slightly lower than the surrounding moorland and is partly submerged under a pool of water.

Inside the Hall large stones were set up on end as a retaining wall and about sixty of these are still in place. With the weathering of the bank behind them, these stones now stand freely, stark and gaunt, making you feel that you are in some primitive temple.

Who were the people who went to this enormous effort? And why did they choose this exposed site on the top of Cornwall? Some say that it was a cattle pound, others a place of assembly, a cockfighting pit, or an earthwork occupied by a small detachment of Roman troops, but we think the most fitting explanation is a monument with ritualistic or burial undertones.

From here the landscape spreads out like a living map: behind you the bare and weathered shoulders of Roughtor and Brownwilly, the highest ground in Cornwall, to the west the cliffs of the North Cornish coast, and away to the south east the lunar terrain of the china clay country around St Austell.

TRETHEVY QUOIT

Now our journey takes us on to St Cleer on the south east of the Moor. St Cleer is one of those Cornish parishes which somehow miraculously still linger in the distant past and probably its most famous inhabitant in the landscape is Trethevy or Arthur's Quoit. Here a giant capstone resting on upright supports forms a Megalithic tomb with two chambers.

Access to the inner tomb is through a small aperture in the stone which is only large enough to crawl through — and there are three fascinating explanations for this tiny entrance: one, to allow the spirit of the departed to go free, two, so that food might be placed there for use in the hereafter and three, to prevent the spirits of the dead escaping. Conflicting perhaps, but interesting.

Belonging to the Megalithic period, this and Zennor are the only surviving Cornish quoits with a brace of chambers. Originally such quoits would have been covered with a cairn mound at least to

▲Trethevy Quoit

Barn with arrow slits at Lantyan▼

the height of the capstone. Perhaps this gives us a clue as to how Neolithic man raised such giant capstones into position.

Looking at a construction like this, you get the feeling that man had little to do with it — almost the notion that it has grown out of the landscape. Something that Dame Barbara Hepworth saw and understood and showed in her sculpture.

CASTLE DORE

As Arthur has been long associated with Tintagel, so this lovely sheltered Fowey region has been linked with King Mark, uncle of Tristan and husband of Iseult. The story of Tristan and Iseult was no doubt handed down by word of mouth for many years before Beroul put pen to paper to preserve for us the earliest known written version. And it was Beroul, writing in the twelfth century, who firmly placed the tale in its Cornish setting.

Originally a story of its own, the Medieval writers, using their imagination, perhaps inevitably married the stories with those of Arthur and the Holy Grail. So, today, you cannot follow Arthur in Cornwall without meeting the ill-fated lovers.

In Beroul's unfinished poem Mark is King of Cornwall and his palace is at Lancien. Lantyan Manor, or Lantien as it was called in Domesday Book, has been a favourite for the siting of this palace by Beroul as has a hamlet called Castle. Lantyan Farm, today is an idyllic spot, set in a green valley. The farmhouse of Lantyan is built of granite, facing a colony of rhododendrons; branches of fantastic shapes stretch, making shadows in the sunlight. But even more interesting is the aged barn with its arrow slits — this must be very old — and according to the present Mrs Santo, the daughter-in-law of the Mr Santo mentioned by Foy Quiller-Couch in her introduction to *Castle Dor*, this has been the suggested site of Mark's Palace. Perhaps this old barn may have been built on even older foundations. On the day we called, a bullock eyed us from a downstairs window, and on the other side we climbed the massive stone staircase to look inside and, in our imagination, see the men and women and animals who have peopled this aged two-storey building.

But it was the excavations in the mid 1930s at Castle Dore that fired the imagination of all those captivated by the Tristan and Iseult

▲Castle Dore   Lantyan Farm today▶

legend. For those expecting another Tintagel, Castle Dore will be a disappointment. There are no crumbling ruins, no dramatic cliffs, for this castle was an Iron Age hillfort not a medieval fortress. Two giant banks with their ditches formed this roughly circular earth-work situated on the ridge along which ran that routeway crossing the Cornish peninsula from the Camel to Fowey. But during these archaeological excavations, many post holes were found, which indicated that a large wooden building had stood within these earth-work defences some fourteen centuries ago. They suggested an imposing aisled hall, with its associated buildings, grand enough to fit the traditional picture of the court of a Celtic King at the time of King Mark, although only a few beads and two fragments of pottery were found to date it to the sixth century. Was this then, Lancien, legendary palace of King Mark? Dr Ralegh Radford, who directed these excavations, certainly thought that this situation, dominating the transpeninsular route, is where one might easily expect to find the seat of the Celtic ruler of South Cornwall in these early times. He also suggested that the Giant's Hedge, a great earth bank which

56

originally ran between Looe and the Lerryn River — only visible in small sections today — could have marked the boundary of his estate.

The love story of Tristan and Iseult must rank among the greatest of its kind in Europe. Tristan was the perfect knight, courteous and accomplished in everything he did, almost too good to be true. The nephew of King Mark of Cornwall, he was sent to Ireland to ask for the hand of Princess Iseult on behalf of the King. On the journey back to Cornwall Tristan and Iseult accidentally shared a love potion intended for the Princess and King Mark on their wedding night. They fell hopelessly and helplessly in love. Iseult became Mark's Queen and the young couple did their best to conceal their love, but the barons, jealous of Tristan's favour at court, were only too keen to betray them. Mark refused to believe the barons, but one day he found the lovers together and in a fit of rage banished Tristan from court. Thereafter life became difficult for the lovers until Tristan devised a clever strategy. The story goes that behind the Palace stood an orchard with a stream which flowed through the Queen's chamber and when the knight wanted to meet his lover he would throw a twig from a linden tree, closely followed by a piece of wood on which a five-pointed cross was scratched. This combination represented a signal and Iseult would come out into the orchard and rendezvous at the spring. Suspicion raised its head again and King Mark was persuaded to climb into a tree and watch the lovers meeting. Luckily for the young couple it was a moonlit night and Iseult saw the shadow of the King reflected in the pool.

But fate could not be kept at bay indefinitely and according to Beroul's version, they were condemned to death. Tristan managed to escape and rescued Iseult.

The Tristan and Iseult legend belongs to Cornwall as naturally as Cornish cream, mead or the pasty. So it was perhaps inevitable that a Cornishman with a creative spirit, like Sir Arthur Quiller-Couch, should decide to resurrect the legend in the Cornwall of the 1800s — not surprising either that he chose as the setting his beloved Fowey, the 'Troy Town' of his other novels. Q's daughter, Foy Quiller-Couch, recalled that he discovered Mark's gate one afternoon in the late 1920s on a local map and she remembered him rowing her up the River Fowey in search of place associations. It was then that the novel *Castle Dor* was conceived. But for some reason he never advanced beyond about the halfway stage of the manuscript, and it did not come to light until his death in 1944. Then in 1959 Miss Quiller-Couch had the bright idea of 'asking my friend Daphne du Maurier to resolve and finish it — no light thing to ask. But she has done it . . .' And so *Castle Dor* saw the light of publication day in 1961 — some forty years after that row up the River Fowey.

Cornwall has inspired finer novels, but Dame Daphne's imagination has completed it — and skilfully. We recommend it as an enjoyable Cornish read: Amyot, the Breton onion-seller, the attractive and newly-wed Linnet Lawharne, and Dr Carfax — who must owe something to Q himself — are just three of the characters in a tale that captures the romantic atmosphere of Lantyan and Castle Dore.

Few writers have the ability and the imagination to resurrect the vanished and *Vanishing Cornwall* as Dame Daphne du Maurier. In the mid 1960s she wrote: 'Castle Dor bears no trace of excavation but has reverted once again to tumbling earth and brambled ditch. This spring the centre of the site, where Mark's Great Hall once stood, some ninety feet long, aisled, with timbered roof and gabled porch, was under plough. All is buried now; stables, granaries, porters' lodges, chieftain's hall lie confused and intermingled with the huts of the Iron Age settlers . . .'

THE TRISTAN STONE

Beyond Castle Dore on the road to Fowey, on the left handside before you start dropping down into the town, you'll find Tristan's Stone. Seven feet tall, this weatherbeaten monolith has a regal quality, and a stranger would choose that word perhaps before even discovering that it once marked the grave of some chieftain or member of a royal family.

It was originally known to stand just to the south of the Castle. The inscription which runs in two lines down one face of the stone, reads: *DRUSTANUS HIC IACIT CUNOMORI FILIUS* meaning 'Here lies Tristan, son of Cunomorus'. Drustanus is the sixth century name for Tristan and Cunomorus, or Cynvawr, interestingly was one of the sixth century kings of Dumnonia — and Cornwall was part of the kingdom of Dumnonia. So we are truly on Royal ground in a sense. Furthermore, in a Breton manuscript of the ninth century,

Cunomorus is given as an alternative name for King Mark.

Although in the surviving legends, Tristan is the nephew of Mark, this stone certainly seems to marry fact and myth in the search for Arthur's Cornwall. At this time it was not uncommon to set up roadside memorial stones in the Roman manner and its original position could well have marked the burial place of a Celtic chieftain.

ST SAMPSON'S CHURCH

The Church of St Sampson stands high above the River Fowey and Golant: a chough's eye view of the graceful river as she flows seaward. There is something special about churches on high ground; perhaps those primitive thoughts about religious buildings were right. A raging storm, they said, was really conflict between the Forces of the Devil and the Heavenly Host and sacred buildings, high up, kept the evil spirits away from the earth. So many headstones proclaim 'Gone but not forgotten', yet many neglected churchyards prove the reverse. Here at St Sampson, either in the lovely churchyard or inside the four walls of the building, you genuinely believe Death is not the end but a door opening.

In this church you feel you're standing amidst history and legend. As far as the legends go, in this romantic spot, the story of Tristan and Iseult somehow takes on a new strength. There are, of course, various versions of this ill-fated triangle. The pamphlet in the Church tells us that when the lovers were discovered in compromising circumstances, Tristan fled to France. There he married another Iseult, the daughter of a French chief. Marriage however could not erase the memory of his Cornish love for the first Iseult; so much so that when Tristan was seriously wounded on a hunting expedition, he sent a message back to Cornwall, asking his first love to come to France to nurse him. He sent a ship, commanding the sailors to hoist black flags if they had failed in their mission, and white if she were aboard with them. His wife, hearing of this arrangement, lied to Tristan saying they had hoisted black flags. Tristan, according to the tale, died, and soon after her arrival from Cornwall, Iseult died too . . . and they were buried alongside one another. Out of their graves saplings grew and, in some magical way, their branches became entwined. So though parted cruelly in Life, Tristan and

Tristan Stone

St Sampson's Church

Iseult were united for ever in Death.

Cornwall has been called the Land of Saints and Sinners, and among the former St Sampson emerges as a strong character. After studying in Ireland and travelling from Wales, St Sampson came to Cornwall, landing at Padstow. He crossed Cornwall at the time of Arthur and Mark by the trade route to the south coast. On the way, the story goes, he found the local inhabitants dancing round a heathen image and he managed to convert them, baptise them and slay a dragon, before continuing on to Golant. Here high above the river he settled, building a shelter close by the well which you'll find near the south door. He is reputed to have been a considerable missionary, and after Cornwall moved on to Brittany where he became an Archbishop.

It was probably at Golant that he founded a monastery and it was no doubt to this monastery that Iseult came to give thanks after her reconciliation with King Mark. Beroul recalls that she rode back to

Lancien, where the bells were ringing and the streets decorated, and up the paved road to the church of St Sampson. Clerics, including the bishop plus the abbot and monks, were there to meet her; and she made her thanks-offering of a splendid robe embroidered with gold and jewels. This was so magnificent that it was made into a chasuble still in use at the time of Beroul. The festivities were such that they even surpassed those on her wedding day.

TRISTAN'S LEAP

Here perhaps we ought to repeat the fact that there are *many* versions of the Arthur and Mark legends.

There may be some difference of opinion about exactly where Tristan leapt to safety, but in Cornwall generally, it is accepted as Chapel Point, the site of an ancient chapel, superbly placed for a

Chapel Point — Tristan's Leap

dangerous escape down the cliff face. You will find Chapel Point further down the Cornish coast between Mevagissey and Gorran Haven. The theory is that Tristan escaped with a truly amazing leap from a chapel window, having deceived his guards who thought that he wanted to pray before his execution. He and Iseult had been finally condemned to death by Mark. The leap seemed an impossibility but Tristan for his part obviously preferred that kind of death to one by burning. Miraculously he escaped death and even more miraculously rescued his beloved.

Another historic event has been added to this piece of Cornish coast, showing how legend breeds legend. Just inland from Chapel Point was the fortified manor home of the Bodrugan family, and it was the last of the Bodrugans, Sir Henry, who also gave the name Bodrugan's Leap to Chapel Point. Having supported the Lambert Simnel rebellion against Henry VII, Sir Henry Bodrugan found himself fleeing from the King's men. The story goes that he rode his horse straight over the cliff, and escaped in a boat to France.

This southern bit of Cornwall may be a world away from Tintagel on the north coast, but it is well worth a visit — however tenuous the Arthurian link — for here as on any Cornish cliff you can lose all sense of time and feel the agelessness and isolation — and the healing qualities.

ROCHE ROCK

Our journey among the legends now moves inland from the sea to the Goss Moors. Again a tenuous link perhaps, but well worth the journey.

When Tristan wished to bring about the reconciliation of Iseult with King Mark, he asked Ogrin the hermit to act as go-between. Now Cornwall has given sanctuary to many a hermit and one of the loveliest and most romantic hermitages which features in many of the County's legends is Roche Rock on the edge of Goss Moor. Ditmas in his book on the Tristan story suggests that Beroul might have been thinking of the hermitage at Roche Rock.

The ruins are still there a hundred feet high crowning a dramatic granite crag, a tower with the hermit's cell below and a chapel

Roche Rock

above. Today's ruins belong to the fifteenth century, but the traditions, of course, are deeper back in time.

MAL PAS

Now in following Mark's footsteps we move further down the County.

Mark and Iseult are reconciled, and Tristan leaves court. But the barons, eager to make trouble tell the King that the people are discontented because Iseult has not cleared herself and they demand a trial by ordeal.

Beroul tells how Iseult makes her bargain with the King — she will

Malpas

stand trial if it can take place at Blancheland and if King Arthur and his knights are invited as witnesses. Immediately, Iseult sends word to Tristan asking him to be at Mal Pas, the place of the marsh where the planks end, on the day of the trial.

There is a Malpas in Cornwall today. It is on the River Fal just below Truro where the creek divides off for Tresillian. High and low water make two very different pictures, for when the water has ebbed wide mud flats stretch between the tree-lined banks, a haven for seabirds and waders of every kind.

Iseult has asked Tristan to come dressed as a leper. Imagine the scene at Mal Pas, the bad place, which has to be crossed to reach Blancheland. Tristan in rough clothes with crutch and clapper, holding out his wooden bowl to beg from all who pass. Gleefully he sends the jealous barons in the wrong direction and they land up in the mud.

But when Iseult arrives in all her finery, she commands the

leper to carry her across. With Iseult on his back, Tristan stumbles over the planks. At Blancheland — in front of all the gathered assembly — Iseult is able to truthfully swear that no man other than her husband King Mark has come between her thighs excepting the leper who carried her over the ford.

LOE POOL

From Mark we now move specifically back to Arthur as we veer south west to Loe Pool.

Some people think Loe Pool, roughly a mile south of Helston, is the more likely setting for both the appearance and disappearance of Arthur's sword, Excalibur. Some versions of the legend have Arthur break the sword he drew from the stone in battle with King Pellinore and therefore Merlin was able to arrange for the Lady of

Loe Pool

the Lake to give Arthur Excalibur.

Wherever it was, Arthur's story fired the imagination of Tennyson whose epic poem *Idylls of the King* will remain one of the landmarks in Arthurian literature.

> *. . . the sword*
> *That rose from out the bosom of the lake,*
> *And Arthur row'd across and took it — rich*
> *With jewels, elfin Urim, on the hilt,*
> *Bewildering heart and eye — the blade so bright*
> *That men are blinded by it . . .*

Loe Pool deserves a visit on any Arthurian excursion across Cornwall, for it's unique. With a bar of gravel and flint, it's the largest lake in all Cornwall, and the Poet Laureate has referred to it as 'a sort of short Chesil Beach with a fresh water lagoon behind it'. The footpath skirting it is open on weekdays. Remember though an old local theory that the Pool claims a victim every seven years, and outside and beyond any Arthurian possibility, there is the tale of a Spanish treasure ship. One stormy day she was driven over the bar and lies — they say — to this day at the bottom and around her wreck

St Michael's Mount

many folktales have grown. Not for nothing is Cornwall known as the land of legend.

And in the legendary landscape of Cornwall, Jan Tregeagle is a recurring giant. We met him at Dozmary Pool on Bodmin Moor . . . Well, he has followed us to Loe Pool. Tregeagle was trudging home one day, carrying a massive sackful of sand on his back, planning to sprinkle it on the floor of his parlour. Passing the top of the hills which today overlook this Pool, he discovered that the Devil was chasing him. Anxious not to be caught, Tregeagle hurriedly opened his sack, shaking the sand over the precipice, between the sea and the river which ran into it — and, in a matter of seconds, the Bar of Loe Pool had been formed — as if by magic. That anyway is how the legend runs.

ST MICHAEL'S MOUNT

Cornish history and legend cannot exclude St Michael's Mount — a romantic island castle and some would say the most beautiful bay in Britain.

Castles are inevitably woven into the Arthurian legend, and in any romantic story of Cornwall St Michael's Mount is a dominant feature, having inspired many. It is Tennyson's imagined isle:

And we came to the Isle of Flowers, their breath met us out on the sea,

for the spring and the middle Summer sat each on the lap of the breeze.

Humphry Davy, arguably the greatest Cornishman of them all, was born only a few miles away at Penzance, and to the young Davy the Mount meant something special. We have Ann Treneer's word for it. 'The Mount to Davy was a visible symbol of romance . . . On a winter morning, when the sun is low, you may see it in a wash of silver. Davy cared for it most by moonlight — it was under the full moon that he was most strongly to feel visitations, feelings of kinship with nature, which he tried to express with all the resources of his youthful art.'

Many high points in our landscape are linked to giant stories and there is a legend about a giant on the Mount. Unfortunately for the Arthurian enthusiasts, Malory used the twin Mount in France, Mont

St Michele, as the setting for the personal battle of King Arthur and the Giant, who had killed so many people. After his triumph King Arthur 'commandeth his cousin Howell that he should ordain for a church to be builded on the same hill in the worship of Saint Michael.'

Arthur interestingly has retained his ideals down the centuries, and people have been talking about him, writing about him and reading about him — and arguing about him — for seven centuries. Back in the Middle Ages, when the stories of Arthur and his Knights of the Round Table were born, they were thought of as real people — and curiously they have never died. In a sentence, they have shown us how to live *well* — in the best sense of the word.

Today, when the anti-hero is often fashionable, Arthur looks and reads like the traditional hero. Maybe to some he's too good to be true: born of the ruling class, skilful in matters of war and, above all, courageous and honourable. It is significant that strong actors like Richard Harris and Richard Burton have played the Arthur role. So though he may seem to be too good to be true, he is strong. Arthur is — and it's difficult not to write of him in the present tense — Arthur is or was a finely balanced character. A formidable fighter, yes, but not a brute like some modern fighters. Arthur may kill, but his killing is for high ideals — as with the giant.

Maybe in looking at Arthur we are looking at society's needs — our own needs — we want *our* hero to rise above ordinary realms of courage, character and physical strength. We clothe him with super-human characteristics.

We need an Arthur, for Arthur, the hero, brings a special something that our society — and probably most societies outside religious orders — lacks. He brings a something that regenerates Life itself. He makes day-to-day living vivid, purposeful — and worthwhile. In history and in fiction — and the line dividing the two is probably thinner and more blurred than we sometimes imagine — the hero offers us a more complete Life.

Physically too painters and illustrators have tended to depict Arthur and his knights as gentlemanly, aristocratic figures. Look, for example, at Sir Galahad by Watts in the Mansell Collection, and you will see heroism and elegance — and in that figure and his grey charger we possibly see the whole thing.

The Mount was an important landmark in that it stood on another vital trade route from the Hayle estuary to Mount's Bay. Therefore

the mainland fairs attracted crowds and generated business and it was to this fair at St Michael's Mount that Ogrin the hermit came, in Beroul's version of the Tristan story, to purchase clothes and a palfrey for Iseult's reconciliation with Mark. The Fair tradition continues with the Corpus Christi Fair at Penzance.

Rising two hundred and thirty feet above the waves of Mounts Bay, St Michael's Mount today is the stately home of the St Aubyns. Built on the site of an old priory, St Michael's Mount inevitably featured in the Civil War, being held by Francis Basset for the King. But with Cromwell's grip tightening and the Royalist's strongholds capitulating, the Mount's fate was sealed on 16 April 1646 when the fortress surrendered to the Parliamentarians. On the same fateful day the Prince with his Council and three hundred Royalist refugees left Scilly for Jersey.

After the Civil War the Mount was bought by John St Aubyn, whose family still live there to this day, though it is now a National Trust property. You can gain access by foot over the causeway at low tide or, during the summer months, by ferry at high tide.

Hard as it is for us to believe nowadays, the Mount was once permanently linked to the mainland. Ancient records tell us that in 1099 and again in 1118 unusually high tides swallowed vast amounts of the shoreline here in West Cornwall but it is known to have been an island at high tide as far back as 300 BC.

High up on the Mount among the roofs and gables of the priory rises a battlemented tower with a turret. Inside, at night, a beacon flamed light for sailors at sea. Known as St Michael's Chair, this too has an aged legend: Whenever a couple were married, it was said the first to sit in it was destined to be 'the master' of the house. It was this legend that inspired Robert Southey to write the ballad of Richard Penlake and his ill-fated wife Rebecca. Ill-fated indeed, for Rebecca, keen to be 'the master', hurried to be first in the chair, but the bells, ringing so loudly, shot her out of the chair — and Richard, on the spot, became an instant widower.

How the Mount got its name is another question of choice, for there are two legends. One says that St Michael once appeared in a vision to a hermit of the Mount, a supernatural event that inspired Milton to produce *The great vision of the guarded mount.* The other declares that St Michael appeared in a vision to a group of fishermen who saw him standing on a rock on the island in 495 — which brings us back to Arthur's time.

St Michael's Mount — home of the St Aubyns

Both versions have a Supernatural quality. Some say the Mount is all that remains of the eastern side of the lost land of Lyonesse. So it is not surprising that we find Merlin here in Mount's Bay.

MERLYN'S ROCK

Merlin's name lives for ever in the shape of a rock just off Mousehole — Mou'zl is the local pronunciation — a fishing village three miles south of Penzance. And there's good reason for his immortality on the Mousehole map, as there's a tradition that the wizard made an astonishing prediction about the area. 'Some strangers will land on the rock of Merlin who will burn Mousehole, Paul, Penzance and Newlyn,' was Merlin's grim forecast. And in 1595 the Spaniards did precisely that. 'It is worthy of remark,' said Camden, the historian, 'that the Spaniards actually landed on a rock called Merlin', which

73

▲Merlyn's Rock, Mousehole . . .

. . . and the Keigwin Arms▶

is spelt with a 'y' in Cornish. The Spaniards, seeking revenge for the defeat of their Armarda, wrought terrible havoc, turning Mousehole into an horrific furnace. Incredibly the Keigwin Arms escaped destruction. Brave Jenkin Keigwin was killed beneath his porch on that fateful morning in 1595 and his sword is now in Penzance Museum.

We can recommend Mousehole as one of the finest villages in Penwith, and though the Keigwin Arms is no longer an inn, it's well worth an outside look; typically Elizabethan with walls four feet thick, the large projecting porch supported by granite pillars.

THE SCILLY ISLES

Our search for Arthur now takes us way out into the Atlantic, twenty eight miles to the west of Land's End to the Scillies. Two of those islands in the group, or islets, are Great and Little Arthur. Now according to legend, Lyonesse was above water in Arthur's reign,

Isles of Scilly: a southern sea at St Mary's . . .

that lost land which has caught the imagination of generations
— some say the Scillies *are* the high peaks of Lyonesse. This lost
land is as much part of Arthur's story as any landscape we have
explored on the mainland. Tristan's father was said to be king of
Lyonesse.

After his last battle with Mordred, Arthur's followers fled west-
wards retreating from Mordred. Once they had passed safely over
Lyonesse, Merlin caused a catastrophic earthquake to engulf
Mordred and his men as the land of Lyonesse was drowned by the
sea and Arthur's followers escaped to Scilly, the Fortunate Isles.

If you sail to Scilly into the setting sun, you will no doubt feel as
we did that this stretch of water is like a moat, separating the world
of everyday from that other magical world.

Legend in Greek and Roman times spoke of a group of islands

beyond the Pillars of Hercules called the Islands of the Blest, where life was idyllic and where heroes were brought to be buried in order to find eternal peace. This idea is presented in Celtic myth and their land of the dead, or Avalon, has been linked with the Scillies, the Land of the Shades, where holy men inhabited the islands and a chief or king could be safely buried and remain in peace.

The large number of chambered barrows of the megalithic period on Scilly seem disproportionate when compared with the number on the mainland in Cornwall and give strength to this idea that the islands were a place of rest for the souls of the exalted.

When Arthur was dying of his wounds after the battle of Camlann, the story goes that Sir Bedivere lay him in a barge at the water's edge and the dying Arthur took leave of him with the words, 'For I must into the vale of Avalon to heal me of my grievous wound. But be you sure that I will come again when the land of Britain has need of me'.

Avalon, in Tennyson's words, was an island-valley.

> *Where falls not hail, or rain, or any snow,*
> *Nor ever wind blows loudly;*

The Scillies, in reality, are made up of five inhabited islands — six, if the Gugh with its one farmhouse is counted as separate from St Agnes — and over one hundred smaller islands and rocks. We have heard it said that there is an island for every day of the year. The largest island is St Mary's, but this is only three miles at the widest and ten miles around its coastline. With its exceptionally mild climate, the Scillies or the Scillonians produce early flowers, the islands' main export, while their main import is the visitor. Scilly's beaches are cleaner than most on the mainland, and many of them are coated in a fine white sand that can glisten like silver.

The magic of a holiday in Scilly is a boat trip to many an un-inhabited island, but as this group is a natural bird sanctuary visitors are encouraged not to land on some off-islands in the breeding season.

Tresco rates itself not only one of the most beautiful in Scilly, but in the whole world. Lying in sheltered, brilliantly coloured water, it is private property without motor cars, boasting internationally known botanical gardens, containing many rare — sub-tropical — plants and trees and a maritime museum of ship's figureheads.

To the south west of Tresco lies Samson Isle — two hills joined by

. . . Little Arthur from Great Arthur

a sandy isthmus. Here too we meet Arthur and once more Tristan. The tradition is that Morholt came to Cornwall to exact tribute for his sister, Queen of Ireland — a human tribute in the form of all the boys and girls aged fifteen. Of all King Mark's Court only Tristan had the courage to stand up to Morholt. First though he had to reveal his identity as the King's nephew in order that Mark should knight him.

The contest between Tristan and Morholt took place on an island 'off the coast of Cornwall' which some versions name the Island of St Samson. It was a long, bloody and desperate battle, and Tristan, though badly wounded in the thigh, ultimately triumphed when he brought his sword down on to Morholt's head, cutting through his helmet and deep into his skull.

If the ghosts of either victor or vanquished lurk on Samson today,

. . . ruined cottage on Samson

they can do no haunting as all the houses have fallen into ruin. But
one ruined cottage by tradition has acquired an immortality — the
house of Armorel, the heroine of *Armorel of Lyonesse,* a novel by
Sir Walter Besant.

But apart from the legend and the history of these islands, there is
a magic in the atmosphere.

When you have left behind the pressures and demands of everyday life — that grosser living that takes so much of our time —
and in your search arrive at these final outposts, there you have to
stay for there is no place beyond. And as you fall under the
spell of these islands, you realise more and more that now there is no
other place to search for the Holy Grail — all our problems have to be
resolved within ourselves.

LAND'S END

Land's End: the very words fire the imagination and there *is* an Arthurian quality about this first and last bit of Cornwall. Charles Dickens said he had known no equal experience to seeing the sun set over Land's End, and though the place may have changed somewhat since Dickens's visit, thousands would echo his opinion today. Land's End, of course, has its critics, and it's fair to say you'll probably enjoy it most when the crowds, the cars and the coaches are not there — or when they're relatively few — but beyond the inevitable amenities for visitors there is still a wild, mysterious something. Naturally if you come in spring or autumn, when you may be lucky enough to have the place more or less to yourself, you will feel its magic most. Yet we have been here, when crowds have been thick, and it's still possible to find Land's End an awe-inspiring experience. Basically it's a matter of only walking a few furlongs — getting away from the congestion.

At Land's End you are standing on the most westerly land in Britain, and by walking east or west you will be meeting some of the most spectacular cliff scenery that you could find anywhere in the world. The colouring too can be brilliant. On a diamond-sharp day the golden and grey cliffs are seen against an emerald sea.

And don't necessarily be put off by what we call 'bad weather', as a stormy day can be a thrilling sight — thrilling anyway viewed from the safety of this natural grandstand. But 'out there' rough weather can be a terrifying experience. There is simply no shelter off Land's End in a storm, and gales and treacherous currents can make a dangerous, even a deadly combination. The seas around this jagged Cornish coastline are littered with wrecks, so it's not surprising that Ruth Manning-Sanders on the twilight of a wintry afternoon reflected: 'It is then that the drowned sailors can be heard "hailing their names" above the moaning of the waters . . . It is then that the place becomes haunted . . .'

It is unwise to be dogmatic about Land's End. There are many moods and shades which can be subtle. The sun setting over the Scillies, flushing crimson in the west or the moon making an oily sea — those are just two totally different but equally beautiful images. Or the regular lights flashing from the lighthouses. The images are various. Out on these cliffs, Lyonesse suddenly becomes

Land's End — on these cliffs . . .

a possibility rather than a piece of fiction.

It's said there were beautiful cities, rich, fertile plains and a noble race of people. One hundred and forty church towers summoned people to prayer. Legend cannot date the disaster when Trevilian — or Trevelyan — escaped on his legendary white horse, the animal carrying him safely before the wall of water. Moreover geology can neither confirm nor deny, and learned scholars, despite their diligent researches, have only been able to wonder. So Lyonesse retains its secret.

The Vyvyans — one of the great Cornish families — of Trelowarren, near Helston, have owned land in Penwith near the Land's End for more than eight centuries, and they still have as their family crest a white horse, saddled but riderless — a perpetual memory of that famous white horse who carried an ancestor to safety

. . . Lyonesse becomes a possibility

from those terrible waves. Moreover the family is said to have kept a white horse in their stables at Trelowarren, saddled and waiting for another such crisis exit. Fortunately he was never needed.

D.H. Lawrence, who loved Cornwall but hated the Cornish, saw Cornwall as a region apart. 'It is not England', he said. 'It is bare and elemental, Tristan's land. I lie looking down a cove where the waves come white under a low, black headland which slopes up in bare green-brown, bare and sand under a level sky. It is old, Celtic, pre-Christian.' And later he wrote: 'It is a cove like Tristan sailed into, from Lyonesse — just the same. It belongs to two thousand years back — that pre-Arthurian Celtic flicker of being which has disappeared so entirely . . . All is desolate and foresaken, not linked up. But I like it.'

Land's End is a must for any Arthurian explorer of Cornwall. If

▲Sevenstones Lightship

The most westerly land in Britain▶

you have the luck to come here as the sun slants westward, you will discover that Land's End is truly a living theatre — a dynamo for the imagination.

In such a setting is there wonder that men and women have argued for centuries about the possibility of Lyonesse? Did Lyonesse once upon a time unite Cornwall and the Scillies?

The death of Lyonesse was no sudden deluge, for the theory behind the escape of one man and his horse was that this ancestor of the Trevilians carefully noted the sea making gradual — albeit dangerous — inroads. His concern was such that he moved his wife, family and cattle inland — and when eventually doom struck in the shape of a flood burst, the white horse and rider galloped to safety, coming ashore at Perran.

No such disaster has been recorded but superstition is strong hereabouts and legends, like old soldiers, never die. Some claim that vegetation washed ashore in Mount's Bay is evidence of that former land, belonging to reality. Others recall Heath's words: '. . . at

Sennen Church Town, near the extremity of Cornwall. There is a base of an old stone-column belonging to a building which was taken up by some fishermen at the Place of the Seven Stones, about eighteen inches high and three feet diameter at the circular base. Besides which, other pieces of buildings and glass windows have been taken up at different times in the same place with divers kind of utensils'.

Again to quote the legend, the site of the once famous city is now marked by the Seven Stones reef, where *Torrey Canyon* met with disaster in 1967. Fishermen, from the distant past, claim to have seen 'the roofs of churches, houses etc,' under the water on clear days or moonlit nights. Some even claimed to have heard ghostly bells tolling. And nobody, of course, can deny that the rock formation of the Land's End and the Scillies have very close parallels.

The Arthurian scholar, Geoffrey Ashe, has said, '. . . much of this fantasy can be dismissed. The question is whether it all can . . .'

Scholars over the ages have debated whether Arthur is fact or fiction. But does it really matter? The Arthur of Camelot belongs first of all to the Medieval bards who made him larger than Life. They wove tales of heroism and chivalry inspiring the feudal knights of their time to uphold the qualities of honour, bravery and loyalty.

But, then, Arthur has always embodied the highest aims of the human spirit, and for many his battles with the Saxon invaders are symbolic of our own battles in life. The search for the Holy Grail is our inner journey.

And if the storytellers down the centuries have used a local stage on which to act out the legends, what better stage than Cornwall?

On our journey we have travelled to places so different, from castle ruins on Tintagel cliffs to an ancient barn on a working farm, from an imposing island castle to a deserted island in the Scillies, from a silent pool on Bodmin Moor to the mudflats of a south coast estuary. These are only some of the pieces in the Arthurian jig-saw puzzle. But all have one thing in common. That Celtic spirit, which conceived the legends, still lives. Frances Bellerby is right. 'The bones of this land are not speechless.' All these places speak to us in their differing tones. They have different mesages for different people — and if

Longships from Land's End▶

you don't believe us, then go to any or all of them and listen for yourself.

Someone asked on this exploration: 'Do you believe in Arthur?'
We had no hesitation. 'Yes, he's still alive today.'

While there is a Cornwall, there will always be an Arthur.

The Search for
the Real Arthur

COLIN WILSON

ARTHUR'S GRAVE

Some time in the latter years of his reign, King Henry the Second, that indefatigable traveller, was making one of his periodic tours of his realm when he stumbled on a most exciting piece of information; he was informed by a Welsh bard, 'a singer of the past', that the grave of the legendary King Arthur was located at Glastonbury, in the grounds of the Abbey, sixteen feet deep. The body had been buried at that depth, said the bard, to protect it from the Saxons, whom Arthur had defeated on so many occasions. The bard even mentioned the precise location of the site — between two 'pyramids'.

This information was of considerable interest to the king. In the reign of his uncle, King Stephen, a Welsh Bishop named Geoffrey of Monmouth had published a remarkable *History of the Kings of Britain* that revealed that King Arthur was one of the greatest empire builders since Julius Caesar. According to Geoffrey, King Arthur had conquered Ireland, Scandinavia and France, and was about to march on Rome when news of rebellion forced him to return to England. Obviously, this Arthur was one of the greatest of Henry the Second's predecessors.

But what really delighted Henry was the news that King Arthur was buried at Glastonbury. For — as absurd as this sounds — there were thousands of people who believed that Arthur was still alive, and might return any day to overthrow these French-speaking descendants of William the Conqueror. Geoffrey of Monmouth had said that Arthur returned to a place called 'Avalon' (whose location was unknown), but made no mention of his death; and legend asserted that he would return in the day of England's need and overthrow the foreigners.

So it was excellent news that Arthur was dead; not only that, but that he was buried in Glastonbury. Glastonbury Abbey was a place that Henry regarded with affection; in fact, he practically owed his throne to the former Abbot, Henry of Blois. So at the first opportun-

◀Tintagel Castle ruins

ity, Henry called on the new Abbot to tell him the good news.

We may suspect that the Abbot was less delighted than Henry expected him to be. Sixteen feet was a long way to dig down . . . and although the finding of Arthur's grave would certainly bring the Abbey great fame, it wasn't of immediate importance. Glastonbury was already one of the richest Abbeys in England; it didn't need any more fame.

Suddenly, all that changed. On 25 May 1184, the Abbey caught fire and was left in ruins. The only cheering thing about it was that an image of Our Lady of Glastonbury had survived the fire undamaged, a miracle that suggested God still had great things in store for the abbey. Henry the Second produced funds to start rebuilding, and many other nobles contributed. In 1190 (or 1191 — the date is uncertain), one of the monks died, and expressed a wish to be buried in the grounds, between two crosses. These crosses stood on top of two marble pillars that tapered towards the top. It may have struck someone that tapering pillars *could* be described as pyramids. At all events, the monks decided they had better explore the ground before burying their deceased brother. So they told the grave diggers to continue digging beyond the normal six feet. And a foot further down, they encountered a stone slab. Was this the entrance to an underground tomb? They prised it up. There was only solid earth underneath. But on its underside, there was a leaden cross, with a Latin inscription. It read: *Hic jacet sepultus inclytus Rex Artorius in insula Avallonia* — 'Here lies buried the renowned King Arthur in the Isle of Avalon'.

They went on digging. It probably took many days, for the grave had to be enlarged as they went deeper. At sixteen feet, just as the old bard had foretold, the mattocks struck against wood. They cleared away the earth, and discovered an enormous coffin, hollowed out of a tree trunk. Inside, they found a huge skeleton of a man. His skull had been smashed by heavy blows. One of the monks saw a lock of yellow hair, and bent over to grab it. It dissolved in his fingers, and the monk toppled into the coffin. It was only later that they identified fragments of a smaller skeleton — a woman's — and realised that Arthur had been buried with his queen, Guinevere . . .

It hardly needs to be said that, from that moment, the Abbey had no trouble in raising funds. King Arthur was famous all over Europe; pilgrims flocked to the Abbey, and their contributions enabled the monks to rebuild on a magnificent scale.

DID ARTHUR REALLY LIVE?

All of which raises an obvious question: was Arthur really buried at Glastonbury? Or was the whole thing a cynically conceived publicity stunt, to raise money for rebuilding the Abbey? This is, for example, the view of Professor R.F. Treharne, of the University of Wales. Yet I am inclined to doubt it. To begin with, the story is told — among others — by the scholar Giraldus Cambrensis — Gerald of Wales — who actually accompanied Henry the Second on his tours. And although Giraldus is capable of embroidering a good story, he seems to be honest: for example, he is one of the very few historians of the period to denounce Geoffrey of Monmouth's history as a pack of lies. (We now know this to be true; but patriotic Englishmen preferred to believe Geoffrey, and continued to do so for many centuries.) Giraldus tells us that he visited the Abbey not long after the discovery, and saw the skeletons, as well as the leaden cross. We know the cross existed — it was still around until the eighteenth century, and a Tudor historian — Camden — published a sketch of it.

Yet even if the skeletons were genuine, the legends of Arthur's conquests were pure invention. Geoffrey of Monmouth was a disgruntled Welshman with a deep nostalgia for the romantic past of the Celtic race. His book contains about as much history as, say, the *Irish Fairy Tales and Legends* of W.B. Yeats; and the spirit behind it is much the same. We know that Geoffrey invented the wizard Merlin — who was based on a northern bard named Myrddin. Is it not, then, conceivable that he also invented Arthur?

This is, in fact, a theory held by a few scholars; and my friend, Dr Harold Phelps, is engaged in writing a book to prove that King Arthur never existed. It may be worth while explaining roughly why he thinks so. The only historian who was a contemporary of Arthur (if he existed) was the monk Gildas, another bitter and disgruntled cleric, who, around 530 AD, wrote a book *Concerning the Ruin and Conquest of Britain*. Gildas tells the story of how Britain came to be overrun by Saxons, and how these Saxons were 'slaughtered' in large numbers at the 'seige of Mount Badonicus', otherwise known as the Battle of Badon. Now in a later history, known as the *British Historical Miscellany*, written in part by a Welsh monk called Nennius, we are told that the Battle of Badon was won by Arthur. In that case, why didn't the monk Gildas mention Arthur? Could it be because Arthur had become the hero of various Welsh poems in the two centuries that elapsed between Gildas and Nennius, and the Welshman Nennius has decided to introduce this legendary hero into his work? This is the view held by the sceptics, and it cannot be positively refuted.

Personally, I cannot accept it. Commonsense tells us that there is no smoke without fire. The other legendary king of romance is Charlemagne, and we know he existed, because he made his mark all over Europe, and there are hundreds of records. Arthur was an obscure British general who lived three hundred years before Charlemagne, in a remote corner of the then-known civilised world, and there are no contemporary records, unless, as is likely, the references in Nennius are quotations from such documents. But the spread of his fame, from Wales to England, then across Europe, suggests that he was a real person. In fact, I find it difficult to call to mind any famous mythical figure who was absolute and pure invention; even Dr Faustus really existed.

So why did Gildas fail to mention his name? The answer seems to lie in the *Life of St Gildas* by Caradoc of Llancarfan, a contemporary of Geoffrey's. Gildas's brother Hueil was a chieftain who fought against Arthur, and who was put to death by him. Understandably, Gildas hated Arthur. Yet Caradoc also mentions that Gildas demanded compensation from Arthur, and that Arthur paid. Also, then when Gildas was living at Glastonbury, Arthur's wife Guinevere was kidnapped by Melwas, King of Somerset, and taken to Glastonbury. Arthur arrived with an army, and Gildas arranged a treaty under which Guinevere was handed over. It seems clear that Gildas and Arthur knew one another, and that Gildas probably regarded him as a militaristic brute. He *had* to mention the famous Battle of Badon, which held back the Saxon advance for fifty years. But he could not bring himself to mention the name of the general who won the battle . . .

WHO WAS ARTHUR?

So who, in fact, was Arthur? In order to understand his role in history, we have to go back to what we know about the beginning of the Dark Ages in Britain. Around 410 AD, the Romans were pulling out of Britain to go to the rescue of the disintegrating Roman empire. A Welsh chieftain named Vortigern declared himself King of Britain. He was an ardent nationalist who was glad to see the Romans go. Other Britons did not agree — among them a chieftain named Ambrosius Aurelianus who, as his name suggests, was thoroughly Romanised. But Ambrosius bided his time.

Vortigern soon found himself in trouble with wild invaders who poured over his northern borders — the Picts. The Saxons were also causing trouble with raids on the southern coast. Vortigern thought he saw a solution: invite the Saxons to settle in England as mercenaries, and get them to beat off the barbarian Scots. At first the plan worked; the Saxons routed the Scots. The trouble was that Vortigern lacked the money to keep on paying them, so the Saxons proceeded to colonise England by means of the sword. Eventually, they drove the Welsh back into Wales, the Scots into Scotland, and the other Celts into Devon and Cornwall — known as the kingdom of Dumnonia. But all this took about two centuries. And their initial success was so tremendous that it seems amazing that it took even two decades.

What happened was that the British rallied. The Saxons swept across Kent, slaughtering all who opposed them; Vortigern's realm collapsed in ruins. But the son of the King of Dumnonia, Ambrosius Aurelianus — the Romanised Celt — decided to resist. He went to war with Roman thoroughness and efficiency, and the Saxons found their advance halted. Other Romanised Britons — and antinationalists — joined Ambrosius. Oddly enough, they regarded themselves as Romans, and Britain as part of the Roman empire.

One of Ambrosius's ablest commanders was a young man named Artorius, which became Anglicised to Arthur. When Ambrosius died, some time before AD 500, Uther Pendragon succeeded him, then Arthur. It was Arthur who stemmed the Saxon advance. And if the Britons had remained united behind Arthur, it is probable that the Saxons would have been pushed back into the sea. In which case I would not be writing this, and most of my readers would not be reading it. For the nation that became the English is a mixture of Saxon and Celtic stock. And the Saxons conquered England only because the Celts were incapable of disciplined unity. As soon as the Saxon tide had been stemmed — at the crucial Battle of Badon — they fell to squabbling amongst themselves. And Arthur spent the

95

rest of his life trying to avoid being stabbed in the back by his own allies. When he finally died, at a battle called Camlann, probably in the area of Hadrian's Wall, he was fighting against his own nephew Mordred, not the Saxon invaders.

That, then, is the basis of the legend of the heroic King Arthur. He was not a king — at least, not at the beginning. He was not even a genuine hereditary noble. He was the Roman general — I say Roman because he thought of himself as a Roman — who rallied the British against Hengist, the leader of the Saxons. He fought the Saxons in twelve battles, which are listed by Nennius. He won them all, which is enough to account for his reputation as a legendary conqueror; but it was not until the twelfth, the Battle of Badon Hill — which lasted for three days — that he inflicted such slaughter on them that they withdrew to lick their wounds for half a century. It was one of those battles that alter the course of history — whichever side happens to win. The Saxons knew that half of Arthur's army was away fighting in the north, and they surrounded him at a Celtic hillfort called Badon — probably Badbury in Wiltshire. But after three days, Arthur's men suddenly charged out, and cut the Saxons to pieces. Thousands of mutilated dead were left on the hillside.

The battle of Badon took place about AD 515. Arthur was then 45 years old, if we accept Mr Geoffrey Ashe's suggestion that he was born around AD 470. He was to live another twenty two years. According to the *British Historical Miscellany* of Nennius, the Battle of Camlann took place in 537. His enemies the Saxons reached Glastonbury about 568. By that time, Arthur's bones had been lying there for three decades . . .

ARTHUR IN CORNWALL

You will have noticed that very little of this story has taken place in Devon or Cornwall. Why, then, are there so many Arthurian sites in the Westcountry? The answer, almost certainly, is that Arthur was a 'Dumnonian'; much of his army must have been composed of the men of Devon and Cornwall. And when he vanished from history — taken secretly from Camlann to Glastonbury to be buried (so that the site of his grave should be unknown to the Saxons) — his fellow

Westcountrymen created legends in which he was still alive. In 1155, a chronicler named Herman of Laon described how he came to Bodmin, and was assured by a Cornishman that Arthur was still alive — his servant and the Cornishman came to blows about it. There seems to be strong evidence that Arthur's main fortress was at Cadbury Hill — from the top of which Glastonbury Tor is clearly visible; but his earlier associations were with the Westcountry. Tintagel Castle — where Geoffrey of Monmouth says he was conceived — was not built until the twelfth century; but there had been a fortified Celtic monastery there, and there is no reason why Bossiney — as it was known then — should not have been the actual place of his birth. Other places mentioned by Geoffrey in connection with Arthur are Dimilioc, now Dimeliock, near St Dennis, Ridcaradoch — Rosecraddock, eighteen miles south-east of Tintagel — and the River Camblanus — the Camel, on which the battle of Camlann is supposed to have taken place. Geoffrey gives the impression that he knows the Westcountry first hand, so he may well have picked up these traditions direct from natives, many of whom believed Arthur was still alive.

But at this point, we have to admit that many of the Arthurian traditions of Cornwall may spring from the later association — in writers like Sir Thomas Malory — of King Arthur with the legend of Tristan and Iseult. The 'Tristan Stone', which stands near Castle Dore, carries a Latin inscription 'Here lies Drustanus, son of Cunomori'. Drustanus is the latinised version of Tristan, while Cunomori is fairly certainly King Cynvawr, a contemporary of Ambrosius; a certain monk named Wrmonoc, who wrote in the ninth century, tell us that Cynvawr and King Mark are the same person. So there *is* some historical evidence that the Tristan legend had its origins in the Fowey area, and Castle Dore could easily have been King Mark's real castle. King Cynvawr seems to have died before Arthur was born, but it is quite possible that his son Tristan fought with Ambrosius against the Saxons, and later with Arthur. Other 'knights of the Round Table' who are actually mentioned in historical chronicles, and who therefore almost certainly existed, are Sir Kay, Sir Bedivere, Mordred, and Sir Gawain (whose Celtic names are Cei, Bedwyr, Medraut and Gwalchmei). Guinevere and Iseult also seem to be historical figures. So on the whole, there is a great deal of evidence for the real existence of Arthur and his knights, and for the two ladies involved. The only thing we have to remember, in trying to picture them, is that they never wore suits of heavy armour with visors — which were not invented until the fourteenth century — but something more like the Roman armour.

EXCALIBUR AND THE HOLY GRAIL

And what of the sword Excalibur and the Holy Grail? These sound purely mythical; yet in his excellent study *Arthur: Roman Britain's Last Champion*, Beram Saklatvala has argued convincingly that both probably existed. The Latin for stone is *saxo*, which is close to 'Saxon'. If some early chronicle mentioned Arthur as taking a sword from a Saxon — some warrior he had killed — then it could well have been the origin of the sword in the stone. Arthur's sword is called Excalibur. *Ex* means 'out of'; Geoffrey of Monmouth calls Arthur's sword 'Caliburn'. And Caliburn is a combination of two words for 'river' — the Celtic *cale* and the Saxon *burn*. Swords need, of course, to be tempered in flowing cold water and, as the Anglo-Saxon word *cale* means cold, so Caliburn could be translated as the 'cold stream'. There *is* a River Cale, that was taken over by the Saxons — it is near Sturminster in Dorset. Arthur's sword was probably called after the river it was tempered in, the Cale. But again, we should bear in mind that it would not be a great war sword, of the kind the knights of the Middle Ages used, but a Roman-type short sword.

As to the Grail — the cup that Jesus was supposed to have used at the Last Supper, and which Joseph of Arimathea is said to have brought to Glastonbury — this was probably a much larger vessel, too large for a drinking cup, that was used for ritual purposes. In 1959, a large marble urn was found during excavations at a Roman palace in North Africa; the place was of the same period as Ambrosius and Arthur. It had a cross carved on it, and the lid also has a cross let into it — rivet holes showing that it once contained a metal cross, probably gold. The urn probably contained the bones of a saint, and was almost certainly used for administering oaths — as we now swear on the Bible. A libation hole also suggests it was used in some special ritual. Arthur would fairly certainly have had a similar urn in his own chapel, for the administering of oaths: after all, he spent much of his life persuading various local chieftains to swear loyalty to him. Arthur's 'Grail' was probably smaller than the

North African reliquary, and the probability is that it came from Glastonbury, where a cup *was* preserved as the actual vessel brought to England by Joseph of Arimathea. It is also important to remember that Arthur fought as a *Christian* king; the Saxons were pagans, and Arthur regarded his fight against them as a kind of crusade. The *Historical Miscellany* says that at the Battle of Badon, Arthur 'carried the cross of our Lord on his shoulders for three days and nights'. 'Shoulders' could here be a mistranslation for 'shield'. Almost certainly, Arthur had a cross on his shield. So the strongly Christian element in the Arthur story certainly has a firm basis in fact. We may also recall that one of the chronicles tells of Arthur beseiging Glastonbury to get Guinevere back from King Melwas. If the local king was at this time hostile to Arthur, he may well have taken the Grail as a spoil of war.

ARTHUR'S CONQUEST

Let me borrow from Saklatvala's summary of the life of Arthur. Born around 570, he grew up as a protégé of King Ambrosius. Ambrosius died when Arthur was about twenty, and Arthur then served for a while under Uther Pendragon. Finally, around AD 512, he took over the leadership of the British resistance against the Saxons. He discarded Uther's dragon emblem and set himself up as the leader of England's Christians — whether British or not — against the pagan invader. Five years later, his tremendous victory at Badon established peace, and Arthur assumed the title of Duke of Britain. He actually married the daughter of a Christianised Saxon, Leodgrance — a girl named Winifred — but her 'foreignness' caused trouble, and he finally sent her back home to her father, and married Guinevere.

But now the Saxons were no longer a menace, Arthur's allies began to squabble among themselves. In the south — particularly Wales and the Westcountry — he remained the almost god-like hero of Badon — much as Montgomery remained the hero of Alamein. But in the north, the chieftains saw no reason to submit to his leadership, and Arthur had to fight some of his battles to subdue them — in one of these, Gildas's brother Hueil was captured and executed. Finally, as he approached his sixties, his treacherous nephew Mordred allied himself with these rebellious chieftains, promising that when he was king, he would be their friend rather than their ruler. To undermine Arthur's authority, the Grail was stolen from his chapel; it was recovered eventually by an officer named Galerius Hadrianus, which was later Anglicised to Galahad. Later, the relic was stolen a second time, and vanished for good. Finally, in 537, the kings of the North, led by Mordred, rose against Arthur. He marched against them and fought his last battle on Hadrian's Wall. Mordred was killed. And the seriously wounded Arthur was taken south, to Glastonbury. Perhaps his commanders hoped that some relic in the holy place might cure him. But Arthur died, and his bones were buried deep, to keep them from desecration in the future by the Saxons.

With Arthur dead, the Saxons again burst out of Kent. With no great leader to unite them, the divided local chieftains were defeated one at a time. Within ten years of his death, the surviving chiefs must have realised that his overthrow was the end of an era — and one of the greatest tragedies to befall the British nation. Twenty years after that, the Saxons marched into Glastonbury. Fortunately, Arthur's grave was unmarked; but the tradition of its existence continued to survive in Wales and Cornwall, where the Celts had retreated in the face of the invader.

But although this new Angle-land had forgotten Arthur, the Celtic bards remembered him. The legends and poems proliferated. And Arthur's real conquest — the conquest of the European imagination — began.

OTHER ARTHURIAN TITLES

The Quest for Arthur's Britain, edited by Geoffrey Ashe, The Pall Mall Press Ltd.

King Arthur & the Grail, Richard Cavendish, Weidenfeld and Nicolson

Arthurian Sites in the West, C.A. Ralegh Radford, Michael J. Swanton, University of Exeter

Le Morte d'Arthur, Thomas Malory

Tristan and Iseult in Cornwall, E.M.R. Ditmas

The Fortunate Islands, R.L. Bowley, Bowley Publications Ltd.

Arthur's Britain, Leslie Alcock, Allen Lane, Penguin Books.

We are indebted to Dame Daphne du Maurier for the quotation on Castle Dore coming from her book *Vanishing Cornwall* published by Victor Gollanz, and to Sir John Betjeman and Faber & Faber for the use of a small extract from the *Shell Guide Cornwall*.

ALSO AVAILABLE

LEGENDS OF CORNWALL
by Sally Jones. 60 photographs and drawings. Price £1.20.
Brilliantly illustrated with photographs and vivid drawings of legendary characters. A journey through the legendary sites of Cornwall, beginning at the Tamar and ending at Land's End.
'Highly readable and beautifully romantic . . . '
Desmond Lyons, Cornwall Courier

BODMIN MOOR
by E.V. Thompson. 45 photographs and map. Price £1.50.
E.V. Thompson, author of the bestselling novel, *Chase the Wind*, set on the eastern slopes of Bodmin Moor, explores the Moor past and present.
'. . . shows the moor in all its aspects; beautiful, harsh, romantic and almost cruel . . . how well he knows the character of the moor.'
The Editor, Cornish Guardian

MY CORNWALL
A personal vision of Cornwall by eleven writers living and working in the county: Daphne du Maurier, Ronald Duncan, James Turner, Angela du Maurier, Jack Clemo, Denys Val Baker, Colin Wilson, C.C. Vyvyan, Arthur Caddick, Michael Williams and Derek Tangye, with reproductions of paintings by Margo Maeckelberghe and photographs by Bryan Russell. Price £1.50.
''An ambitious collection of chapters.''
The Times, London

CORNWALL & SCILLY PECULIAR
by David Mudd, 48 photographs. Price £1.00.
David Mudd uses his perceptive eye and his pride of all things Cornish to write entertainingly, at times with humour, but always affectionately, of some of the people, events, values and beliefs that create the background to Cornwall's strange and compelling charm.
'. . . one of the most important Cornish titles produced by Bossiney . . . '
The Cornishman

HAWKER COUNTRY

by Joan Rendell. 40 photographs, letters and map. Price £1.20.
Hawker Country is an area of North Cornwall, embracing some cruel, dramatic coastline and beautiful countryside: a corner of the Westcountry immortalised by the great Parson Hawker of Morwenstow.

'. . . a book about that Prince of clerical eccentrics and the places associated with him . . . contains many pictures of great interest.'   The Church Times

OCCULT IN THE WEST

by Michael Williams. Over 30 photographs. Price £1.50.
Michael Williams follows his successful *Supernatural in Cornwall* with further interviews and investigations into the Occult; this time incorporating Devon. Ghosts and clairvoyancy, dreams and psychic painting, healing and hypnosis are only some of the facets of a fascinating story.

'. . . provides the doubters with much food for thought.'
Jean Kenzie, Tavistock Gazette

SUPERNATURAL IN CORNWALL

by Michael Williams, 24 photographs. Price £1.50.

''. . . a book of fact, not fiction . . . covers not only apparitions, and things that go bump in the night, but also witchcraft, clairvoyancy, spiritual healing, even wart charming . . .'   Jenny Myerscough on BBC

''Serious students of ghost-hunting will find a fund of locations.''
Graham Danton on Westward TV

MAKING POLDARK

by Robin Ellis. Over 60 photographs. Price 75p.
The inside story of the popular BBC TV series.

''. . . an interesting insight into the making of the TV series . . .''
Camborne Redruth Packet

''It is a 'proper job', as they say, and a credit to all concerned.''
Archer in Cornwall Courier

DEVON MYSTERIES

by Judy Chard. 22 photographs. Price £1.
Devon is not only a beautiful county, it's a mysterious place too — and if anybody has any doubts about that, Judy Chard demolishes them with her exploration into the strange and often the inexplicable. This book though is not just about *mysterious Devon*, it's essentially about *Devon mysteries*.

'. . . my appetite for unexplained happenings has been truly whetted by Newton Abbot author Judy Chard's latest offering.'   Mid-Devon Advertiser

OTHER TITLES INCLUDE

FOLLOWING THE RIVER FOWEY
by Sarah Foot £1

DOWNALONG CAMBORNE & REDRUTH
by David Mudd   95p

THE FALMOUTH PACKETS
by David Mudd   75p

ABOUT THE CITY
by David Mudd   90p

ABOUT LOOE
by Austin Toms and Brenda Duxbury   75p

HELSTON FLORA DAY
by Jill Newton   60p

ALONG THE DART
by Judy Chard   75p

ALONG THE CAMEL
by Brenda Duxbury & Michael Williams 60p

AROUND & ABOUT THE ROSELAND
by David Mudd £1.20

ABOUT MEVAGISSEY
by Brenda Duxbury 75p

HOME ALONG FALMOUTH & PENRYN
by David Mudd £1.50

PENZANCE TO LAND'S END
by Michael Williams & John Chard 75p